Conflicts Under the Nuclear Umbrella

Indian and Pakistani
Lessons from the
Kargil Crisis

Ashley J. Tellis
C. Christine Fair
Jamison Jo Medby

Prepared for the
United States Communication Agency

National Security Research Division

RAND

This research was conducted within the International Security and Defense Policy Center (ISDPC) of RAND's National Security Research Division (NSRD). NSRD conducts research and analysis for the Office of the Secretary of Defense, the Joint Staff, the Unified Commands, the defense agencies, the Department of the Navy, the U.S. intelligence community, allied foreign governments, and foundations.

Library of Congress Cataloging-in-Publication Data

Tellis, Ashley J.
    Limited conflicts under the nuclear umbrella : Indian and Pakistani lessons
  from the Kargil crisis / Ashley J. Tellis, C. Christine Fair, Jamison Jo Medby.
        p. cm.
    Includes bibliographical references.
    "MR-1450."
    ISBN 0-8330-3101-5
    1. Kargil (India)—History, Military—20th century. 2. Jammu and Kashmir
(India)—Politics and government—20th century. 3. India—Military relations—
Pakistan. 4. Pakistan—Military relations—India. I. Fair, C. Christine. II. Medby,
Jamison Jo. III. Title.

    DS486.K3347 T45 2001
    327.5491054—dc21

                                                              2001048907

RAND is a nonprofit institution that helps improve policy and decisionmaking through research and analysis. RAND® is a registered trademark. RAND's publications do not necessarily reflect the opinions or policies of its research sponsors.

Published 2001 by RAND
1700 Main Street, P.O. Box 2138, Santa Monica, CA 90407-2138
1200 South Hayes Street, Arlington, VA 22202-5050
201 North Craig Street, Suite 102, Pittsburgh, PA 15213
RAND URL: http://www.rand.org/
To order RAND documents or to obtain additional information, contact
Distribution Services: Telephone: (310) 451-7002;
Fax: (310) 451-6915; Email: order@rand.org

This report presents the results of a quick-turnaround study conducted by RAND at the request of the U.S. government in the months leading up to the November 2000 presidential election in the United States. The study was intended to support a variety of internal reviews and briefings that took place around the time of the election.

The broad purpose of the study was to understand how India and Pakistan viewed the significance of the Kargil conflict, what lessons they drew from this conflict, and the implications of those lessons for future stability in South Asia. Consequently, this report is not an all-source document: it has deliberately avoided the use of all U.S. governmental documents and for most part many other open-source American materials as well. Instead, the source materials used are almost exclusively Indian and Pakistani.

Since the significance of the Kargil conflict as appreciated in India and Pakistan is a complex matter, with many different and often conflicting strands of opinion, this report focuses mainly on capturing thematically the dominant ideas circulating in the subcontinent on this issue. As a result, not every view pertaining to Kargil is recorded and, further, many nuances and variations on the main themes recorded here are excluded unless judged by the authors to represent viewpoints that ought to be of interest to policymakers in the United States.

It was initially intended that the lessons learned by India and Pakistan in regard to Kargil would be published separately, but the interesting symmetries in the perceptions of the two sides that were discovered during the course of the research and interviews ultimately justified a unified publication.

This report is by no means intended to be the final word on Indian and Pakistani assessments about Kargil. In fact, it explicitly represents an early view of this issue, since Indian and Pakistani judgments may themselves evolve with time. As official documents on the conflict come to light, more systematic research on some of the key issues touched on in this report—the genesis of the conflict; the character of the operations; the perceptions, judgments, and decisions of the national leaderships; the significance of nuclear weapons; and the role of outside powers—will be possible, and more considered conclusions may be derived. Until that time, however, this preliminary assessment is offered for public consumption in the hope that it will contribute to a better understanding of the problems of stability in South Asia.

The information cutoff date for the material used in this report was March 2001. No effort has been made to update the analysis to account for events occurring after this date, for two reasons. First, any effort of this sort risks being overtaken by events, and second, updating the study would not have advanced the original objective of the U.S. government, which was to assess Indian and Pakistani perceptions in the aftermath of the Kargil war rather than to provide real-time analysis of changing India-Pakistan relations. Consequently, this analysis serves as a benchmark permitting the reader to assess how India-Pakistan relations have changed subsequent to our evaluation.

This research was conducted within the International Security and Defense Policy Center (ISDPC) of RAND's National Security Research Division (NSRD). NSRD conducts research and analysis for the Office of the Secretary of Defense, the Joint Staff, the Unified Commands, the defense agencies, the Department of the Navy, the U.S. intelligence community, allied foreign governments, and foundations.

CONTENTS

In spring 1999, details of the "Kargil conflict"—the latest chapter in the long-standing India-Pakistan dispute over Kashmir—emerged publicly. For these two largest South Asian states, this conflict represents a watershed, in part because it demonstrated that even the presence of nuclear weapons might not appreciably dampen the India-Pakistan security competition.

The goal of this analysis was to assess both combatants' perceptions of the Kargil crisis with a view to evaluating the possibilities for future Kargil-like events. Kargil represented a departure from the low intensity combat (LIC) operations that have most recently typified the military dimension of the Kashmir dispute. Whereas these types of operations typically pit insurgents against Indian police and paramilitary forces, Kargil saw both sides engage with regular military forces across a de facto border in the face of Pakistani attempts to seize and hold territory. The lessons both belligerents took from the crisis and their respective judgments of whether their actions were successful could suggest the prospects for future military actions of greater intensity.

SIGNIFICANCE OF THE KARGIL CRISIS

The crisis is significant at several levels for both Pakistan and India. For Pakistan, it reconfirmed LIC as a legitimate tool for attaining political goals, but it probably also caused the Pakistani leadership to conclude that Kargil-like operations are not legitimate in the current international environment. Moreover, Kargil stands as yet another symbol of the failure of Pakistan's grand strategy and illustrates Islamabad's inability to anticipate the international opprobrium and isolation that ensued from its actions in Kargil. In addition, the crisis posed real concerns about the possibility of the conflict widening to conventional warfare and subsequently escalating to nuclear use.

For India, Kargil confirmed its belief that Pakistan is a reckless, adventuristic, and untrustworthy state. Kargil motivated India to reconsider whether to engage Pakistan diplomatically on the Kashmir issue. In addition, the crisis strengthened the widespread perception that India's intelligence infrastructure has endemic deficiencies. It also led India to realize that international attention to Kashmir is not altogether undesirable, particularly when the attention focuses on Pakistani misadventures.

LESSONS LEARNED FROM THE KARGIL CRISIS

The most important lesson Pakistan took from the crisis was that Kargil-like operations have high political costs, especially for Pakistan's international reputation. That said, the Kargil fiasco does not appear to have extinguished Pakistan's belief that violence, especially as represented by LIC, remains the best policy for pressuring India on Kashmir and other outstanding disputes. While vocal criticisms of the Kargil misadventure are plentiful, there are many stakeholders in Pakistan who view Kargil as some sort of a victory lost. If such beliefs of Kargil—despite being fundamentally false in their details—represent the considered assessments of Pakistan's security managers, future policies could emerge that call for Kargil-like operations. A reemergence of such policies could have disastrous consequences for stability in South Asia.

The most important lesson learned by India was that it must be prepared to counter a wide range of Pakistani threats that may be mounted by what is essentially a reckless but tenacious adversary. India must therefore develop the robust capabilities it needs to thwart surprise and to win even if surprised by Pakistan. Another lesson is that if India is obliged to respond forcefully in future episodes, covert rather than overt action may be preferable.

OPTIONS FOR THE FUTURE

The Kargil conflict has shaped Pakistan's and India's conceptions of their future choices. Pakistan has slowly come to appreciate the costs it has endured as a result of Kargil: Pakistan is economically vulnerable, politically unstable, and internationally isolated; and it is widely viewed as a precarious, decaying, and increasingly Islamist state. As a result, many in the political classes have come to recognize that they must decide among themselves what kind of a state they want to become: Jinnah's Pakistan, the Jamaat-e-Islami's Pakistan, or the Lashkar-e-Taiba's Pakistan.

For its part, India is not likely to give Pakistan a chance to flirt with Kargil-like scenarios again. New Delhi will watch the border in Kashmir and elsewhere carefully and redouble its efforts to prevent infiltration of the sort that occurred at Kargil. India understands that the most likely strategy for Pakistan will be increasing its support for insurgency and for terrorist attacks throughout India. New Delhi also appreciates that this strategy is to Pakistan's own disadvantage and further confirms Islamabad as a sponsor of Islamist terrorism. Despite the episodic temptation to bloody the Pakistani nose, India will continue to exhibit restraint.

CONCLUSIONS

"Ugly stability"—the persistence of unconventional conflicts—will probably endure in the region. State-sponsored terrorism will remain an attractive mode of operation in large part because conventional conflicts remain risky.

Pakistan's evaluation of Kargil's consequences is still ambiguous. In some circles, Kargil may be rationalized into an attractive mode of LIC. However, there are those within Pakistan who have increasingly come to question the costs that Pakistan's LIC strategy has imposed upon the state's economic, social, and political development. Nevertheless, Islamabad remains passionately focused on "resolving" Kashmir, and its support for the insurgency is unlikely to dissipate any time soon.

On its side, India remains committed to an internal solution of the Kashmir problem. India's conviction rests on its larger beliefs about the liberal, secular, and multiethnic nature of the Indian Union, but this conviction has unintendedly increased Pakistan's resistance to an internal solution.

Even if operations on the scale of Kargil do not occur, political-military crises in South Asia are likely to surface over the course of the next decade. Until Pakistan pulls out of its current economic morass, institutionalizes a stable set of responsive governing institutions, develops a democratic temper, cements a political identity outside of its opposition to India, and acts upon the realization that Kashmir—no matter how valuable—is still not as valuable as Pakistan, the resentment, grievances, and dissatisfaction currently driving Islamabad's policies will only compel Pakistan to contemplate future Kargil-like operations.

ACKNOWLEDGMENTS

The authors are grateful, first and foremost, to numerous high-level Indian and Pakistani policymakers, politicians, civil servants, military and intelligence officers (both serving and retired), academics, journalists, and commentators who gave generously of their time and insights to us in November and December 2000. Several U.S. government officials and analysts within the intelligence and policy communities also took the time to discuss key issues pertaining to this study with the authors. In addition, Colonel Jack Gill of the Near East–South Asia Center for Strategic Studies, National Defense University, provided an invaluable detailed critique of the first draft. Their keen eyes saved the authors much embarrassment. The authors are also deeply indebted to John Edward Peters, who crafted a very thoughtful summary for this report. His contribution was critical to completing the report in a timely fashion.

INITIALISMS

APHC	All Parties Hurriyat Conference
COIN	counterinsurgency
HRCP	Human Rights Commission of Pakistan
IAF	Indian Air Force
IMF	International Monetary Fund
ISI	Inter-Service Intelligence (Directorate)
IT	information technology
LIC	low intensity conflict
LOC	line of control
NLI	Northern Light Infantry
NSC	National Security Council
OIC	Organization of Islamic Countries
R&AW	Research and Analysis Wing
UAV	unmanned aerial vehicle
UN	United Nations
U.S.	United States
WMD	weapons of mass destruction

Chapter One

INTRODUCTION

In the spring of 1999, the world slowly came to know of Pakistan's foray into the Kargil-Dras sector in a limited war that has come to be known as the "Kargil conflict." (India's military response to this Pakistani adventure was codenamed OPERATION VIJAY.) Although the "real" reasons for Pakistan's prosecution of the Kargil war cannot be discerned with any certainty right now, a variety of Pakistani writings and public statements suggest that Islamabad likely had several motivations: a desire to redeem itself after its humiliating defeat in the 1971 war with India; India's occupation of the Siachen glacier; a desire to punish India for its periodic shelling of the Neelum Valley road and its other "provocations" along the line of control (LOC) in Kashmir; a desire to energize what at that point appeared to be a flagging insurgency in the Kashmir valley; and, finally, a desire to exploit its newly confirmed nuclear capabilities to achieve those lasting political changes in Kashmir that had hitherto eluded Islamabad.

The Kargil crisis represents a watershed in India-Pakistan security relations. It demonstrated that even the presence of nuclear weapons might not appreciably dampen security competition between the region's largest states. However, it remains an empirical question whether or not the Kargil war represents a foretaste of future episodes of attempted nuclear coercion if India and Pakistan believe that their nuclear capabilities provide them the immunity required to prosecute a range of military operations short of all-out war. Whether one side or both will act upon this belief depends in part on the particular conclusions and lessons they drew from the Kargil conflict.

The goal of this analysis is to assess both combatants' perceptions of the Kargil crisis with a view to evaluating the possibilities of future Kargil-like events. To do so, we first elaborate the significance of the Kargil crisis from the perspective of each country. Second, we explore what key constituencies on both sides learned from the conflict and its aftermath. For example, what strategic and tactical lessons did the Indian and Pakistani military leadership draw? What did each country's intelligence systems learn? What did the political leadership (both the government and opposition parties) in the two countries learn? How did the populaces respond to the crisis and how have their positions evolved? Will these popular perceptions influence the future taste for war and/or war-like operations? Finally, having laid this groundwork, we elaborate for both combatants some of the possible future options, which may or may not include Kargil-like scenarios.

METHODOLOGY

To answer the questions posed above, we conducted exhaustive literature surveys of the popular press and academic literature. Our review of the popular press tended to focus upon May to September 1999, the period over which the conflict occurred.[1] This effort mostly relied upon the English media, for two main reasons. First, the vernacular press represents extreme views that are considerably at variance with those of the English press and often of little help to policymakers in the United States, South Asia, and elsewhere. The Urdu press in Pakistan is particularly vulnerable to this characterization. Second, there is the question of which vernacular press to use, especially in India, where the numerous vernaculars all reflect their own regional and local biases. Where possible, heavy use was made of electronic sources such as the Foreign Broadcast Information Service (FBIS) and the archives maintained by the Institute of Peace and Conflict Studies (New Delhi, India) on Indian and Pakistani media coverage during Kargil. Unfortunately, there is no such electronic archive maintained by any Pakistani institution. As the Pakistani

---

[1]It is important to note that in the two years that have passed since the Kargil crisis, popular opinion may very well have shifted in both countries. A historical review of how popular opinion has changed over the course of this period unfortunately was beyond the scope of this effort.

papers represented in this archive tended to be from the Punjab, a region that is typically less critical of the government, we augmented this archive with a separate review of the Karachi-based newspaper, *The Dawn*. In selecting passages to quote, we often chose the most lucid view of a particular issue, which in the case of Pakistan often occurred in *The Dawn*. Thus, the reader should be cautioned that the citation base does not fully represent the comprehensiveness of the literature review efforts.

In addition to undertaking extensive literature reviews, in November and December 2000 we interviewed several key individuals from both India and Pakistan who are representative of the following constituencies:

- Serving military

- Retired military

- Leadership of principal political parties

- Non-state actors in Pakistan

- Civil servants and retired diplomats

- Media and public commentators

- Researchers at universities and think tanks

One of the interesting analytical problems that arose in explicating Pakistan's perception stemmed from the disparity between information provided during interviews and evidence gathered from the Pakistani popular and academic press. Most contemporary Pakistani accounts of Kargil deny any direct role of the Pakistani Army apart from close support behind the LOC and are thus manifestly incongruent with the accounts published outside of Pakistan. Retired military officers and diplomats, academics, and journalists appeared to be rehearsing the government's version of events when writing in the editorial pages of major newspapers, but generally spoke quite frankly of the Army's involvement during our confidential interviews.

There are several possible explanations for these contradictions. One is that when the story of the occupation first broke in Pakistan, there was very little information available. The Foreign Office account was carried generally without question through most of the conflict. Journalists and private individuals began writing op-ed pieces that obliquely challenged the government's version of events beginning mid- to late-July 1999. More candid rejections of the government's narrative occurred well after the crisis ended. Thus, the differences between the written accounts during the conflict and the interviews in the winter of 2000 may simply reflect an expanded access to information. Alternatively, the differences between public and private accounts may reflect the political stakes of the authors and deference to possible reprisals. Of course, a combination of both factors may account for the differences between public and private narratives of the crisis.

Thus, in this analysis we draw upon both sources of data for Pakistan and note their vastly different perspectives where appropriate. This problem did not arise in the Indian data. Generally, the Indian views obtained in personal interviews were consistent with views expressed in the public domain.

REPORT ORGANIZATION

The remainder of this report is organized as follows. The significance of Kargil for both countries is described in Chapter Two. In Chapter Three, the political, military, and diplomatic lessons learned by both combatants are identified. Chapter Four explores some of the future options as perceived by various stakeholders in India and Pakistan. Finally, Chapter Five presents analyses of the impact of the Kargil crisis on nuclear deterrence stability and identifies several important analytical issues that merit further examination.

Chapter Two

THE SIGNIFICANCE OF THE KARGIL CRISIS

The Kargil crisis had several layers of significance for both Pakistan and India, and generally these were very different for the two countries. For Pakistan, Kargil was significant primarily for the following reasons:

- While Pakistan appears to have concluded that Kargil-like[1] operations are not legitimate in the current international environment, violence in the form of low intensity conflict (LIC) continues to be seen as a legitimate tool for attaining political objectives.[i]

- Kargil was yet another example of the failure of Pakistan's grand strategy. In Kargil, as in the 1965 and 1971 wars, Pakistan failed to comprehend that the international environment would not support its position and consequently did not anticipate or plan for the unanimous international opprobrium and isolation that ensued.

---

[1]In this report, a distinction is generally made between LIC and "Kargil-like" operations. In LIC, which regularly takes place in Kashmir, India confronts irregular forces, such as the mujahideen, and typically uses paramilitary or police forces for such operations. Moreover, LIC operations have generally taken place only in India, particularly in Jammu and Kashmir. Kargil was a departure from such LIC operations in several respects. First, both sides used regular forces in combat. Second, the conflict involved struggles over territory. Third, the scale of military operations was substantially different in that widespread use of heavy artillery and air power was witnessed during the conflict.

- Both the scale of Pakistan's covert operation and the rapidity and degree of India's counter-response were unprecedented in the history of the "violent peace" in Kashmir.

- For many, the Kargil crisis seemed to pose real concerns about the possibility of the conflict widening to conventional war and subsequently escalating to nuclear use.

For India, Kargil was significant for very different reasons:

- India confirmed its belief that Pakistan is a reckless, adventuristic, risk-acceptant, untrustworthy state. Moreover, the Pakistani military came to be seen as a substantial cause of the problems in India-Pakistan relations, as it is understood to be the real power in Pakistan that also happens to be virulently anti-India.

- Kargil motivated India to reconsider whether to engage Pakistan diplomatically on the Kashmir issue. Any Indian inclination to resolve the Kashmir problem with an acknowledgment of Pakistan's equity, in the manner desired by Islamabad, has been vitiated.

- Kargil strengthened the widespread perception that India's intelligence infrastructure has endemic deficiencies. It has reinforced the Indian commitment to a more robust forward defense and to improving logistics and intelligence capabilities to prevent future Pakistani incursions.

- India realized that international attention to Kashmir is not altogether undesirable, particularly when such attention focuses on Pakistani misadventures. India, however, will resist international involvement in the final disposition of Kashmir, particularly if such involvement is directed toward "new map-making" in the disputed state.

- Kargil was India's first televised war. India dexterously made use of the media to shape domestic and international response in its favor.

The next two sections explore the ways in which Pakistan and India perceived the import of the Kargil crisis.

PAKISTAN'S PERSPECTIVE

Kargil-like Operations Are Disavowed, But Violence Remains a Legitimate Tool to Achieve Political Objectives

One of the principal findings of this analysis is that while there is broad consensus that Kargil-like operations are not viable in the current international environment, violence in various forms remains a legitimate—if not the only—means to achieve Pakistan's political objectives in Kashmir. As will be explicated in greater detail later, Pakistan understands that it paid heavily for its adventurism in Kargil and that the international community will not support the use of overt force to alter the status quo. Stated more precisely, Islamabad has concluded that the use of *Pakistani* troops in Kargil invited political failure, and consequently its incentive to repeat such an operation is very small at present.

This does not imply, however, that Pakistan has concluded that other forms of violence are either illegitimate or ineffective for altering the status quo. Pakistan perceives its diplomatic and military options to be quite limited as far as resolving the issue of Kashmir is concerned. Given these constraints, Pakistan believes that one of its few remaining *successful* strategies is to "calibrate" the heat of the insurgency in Kashmir and possibly pressure India through the expansion of violence in other portions of India's territory. Security managers and analysts widely concur that Pakistan will continue to support insurgency in Kashmir, and some have suggested it could extend such operations to other parts of India. It may be inferred that Pakistan has a range of tactical choices for doing so: it can encourage some or all of the jihadi forces (whether Pakistan-based "guest militants" or indigenous Kashmiri groups) to limit their operations to Kashmir alone or to extend them to other parts of India; it can continue to encourage Pakistan's social forces, such as the Jamaat-e-Islami, to spearhead operations within India while leaving the Pakistani state to concentrate on diplomatic activities relating to Kashmir; or it can focus entirely on state-run and state-managed covert operations (in Kashmir and/or throughout India), leaving substate groups in Pakistan essentially on their own.

Failure of Grand Strategy Coupled with Surprise and Shock at International Isolation

Several issues loom large when the significance of Kargil for Pakistan is explicated. Most notably, Pakistani informants and public opinion shapers expressed varying degrees of surprise at the international response to Kargil and the nearly unanimous conviction that Pakistan was culpable. However, the ways in which this surprise was rationalized depended greatly upon how much these people knew about the Pakistani Army's direct role in the operation.

The analysts, retired army officers, diplomats, and journalists who knew of the Army's involvement argued that Pakistan's security managers were surprised in part because they did not perceive a difference between Pakistan's doings and India's violations of both the LOC and the Shimla Agreement, of which Siachen is viewed as the most egregious example. Another, less salient justification for their surprise was the expectation that the international community would be sympathetic to Pakistan's moral claims owing to India's human rights abuses and other excesses in Kashmir. Those who conceded the Army's role in Kargil but did not think that Kargil necessarily undermined the process of engagement represented by the Lahore Declaration articulated a third reason for surprise at Pakistan's isolation. These individuals argued that the Lahore Declaration was designed for the consumption of the international community, which was still rankled by the 1998 nuclear tests in South Asia, and was at any rate derailed by Indian statements in the aftermath of Prime Minister Atal Behari Vajpayee's return to New Delhi.[2] Thus, these interlocutors sought to dismiss the widely held beliefs that Pakistan's operations in Kargil exemplified Pakistani duplicity and that Pakistan had in fact sabotaged the much-acclaimed bus diplomacy and the resultant Lahore Declaration.

---

[2]Upon returning to New Delhi, Prime Minister Vajpayee remarked at a public function, "We have not attacked any country in our 50 years of independence, but we have been attacked several times and lost our land. . . .We are determined not to lose our land in the future." This was read by Pakistan as a clear signal that India would be unwilling to cede territory on the Kashmir issue and as a clear retrenchment from progress made at Lahore the week before. Consequently, Prime Minister Sharif reportedly threatened to break off bilateral talks over Kashmir. (See, for example, "India Determined Not to Lose More Territory: PM," *The Times of India*, March 1, 1999.)

The surprise and alienation felt by members of the Pakistani elite are confirmed by a reading of Pakistan's English-language press, which strongly suggests that at the time of the conflict, editorialists and other opinion shapers did not know that the incursions around Kargil were *not* a mujahideen operation. The surprise evinced in such editorials seems to stem from the writers' beliefs that Kargil was not Pakistan's doing and that Islamabad therefore did not deserve the opprobrium it received.

In the aftermath of the G-8 communiqué,[3] which Pakistanis read as laying the blame squarely on Pakistan, several articles spoke out against what was perceived as an unreasonable and unfair interpretation of events by the international community.[4] One article poignantly narrates Pakistan's sense of loss, isolation, and surprise:

> We have come a long way indeed from the time when the world listened to our entreaties on Kashmir with a certain amount of respect. We have come a long way from the time that the OIC [Organization of Islamic Countries] passed a unanimous resolution on allowing the Kashmiris the right of self-determination. We have come a long way indeed from the time that our protector and giver of all, Amreeka Bahadur, was getting ready to mediate between India and Pakistan. . . .Whatever happened to us? Why do we stand at the very edge of the diplomatic precipice today?[5]

To illuminate Pakistan's current standing in the comity of nations, the author of this article critically examined some of Pakistan's more alienating policies, such as its ongoing support for the Taliban.

The editorial pages also suggested a widespread conviction that China was the last possible bastion of support. An editorial in *The Dawn* compared this anticipated Chinese position to the emergent U.S. position:

---

[3]This June 21, 1999, communiqué articulated the G-8 position on the resolution of the Kargil crisis.

[4]See, for example, "A One Side Approach Will Not Work," *The Dawn*, June 26, 1999; Abbas Rashid, "Raising the Ante in Kashmir," *The News International Pakistan*, July 2, 1999; Dr. Manzur Ejaz, "An Unlikely Beneficiary of the Kargil Crisis," *The News International Pakistan*, July 11, 1999.

[5]Kamram Shafi, "Friendless in Kashmir," *The News International Pakistan*, June 21, 1999.

> [T]he United States has proved to be a fair-weather friend. . . .Instead of showing greater understanding of Pakistan's point of view and impressing upon India the need to discuss the Kashmir problem . . ., the US is telling Pakistan to effect a withdrawal of the Mujahideen (or the infiltrators, as the US prefers to call them) from Kargil. China does not suffer from the same attitude and its understanding of the Pakistani position on all important matters of national security has always been fair and sympathetic.[6]

While such writers persisted optimistically in the days immediately preceding Pakistani Prime Minister Nawaz Sharif's visit to China, others sought to dampen any expectation that China would enthusiastically support Pakistan.[7] These articles typically reaffirmed the general contours of Sino-Pakistan relations while vitiating any expectation that China would be totally forthcoming in assistance. A common strategy employed was to contextualize China's expected stance on Kargil vis-à-vis China's other pressing objectives (e.g., economic, social, and military development).[8]

Of course, the eventual position taken by China did not live up to any of Pakistan's highest expectations. In the days and weeks after the disappointing visits to China by Foreign Minister Sartaj Aziz and then Prime Minister Nawaz Sharif, there was palpable shock at China's position and vexation with the Pakistani Foreign Office's efforts to spin these visits as fruitful. Abbas Rashid's opinion piece typifies this sentiment:

> Even China seems to have forsaken its traditional subtlety to get across the message as plainly as possible that it did not support Pakistan's position. . . .Sartaj Aziz dashed off to Beijing and was reportedly told by Li Peng . . . that '. . . Pakistan should remain cool-headed and exercise self-control and solve conflicts through peaceful means and avoid worsening the situation.'. . .Certainly, this is

---

[6]"PM's China Visit" [editorial], *The Dawn*, June 29, 1999.

[7]See Afzal Mahmood, "Ties with China in Perspective," *The Dawn*, June 29, 1999; Afzal Mahmood, "China's Cautious Approach," *The Dawn*, July 4, 1999; Tanvir Ahmed Khan, "Understanding China Is Vital," *The Dawn*, July 6, 1999; Mayed Ali, "China Pledges to Stand by Pakistan in All Circumstances," *The News*, June 30, 1999.

[8]See "Hope in China" [editorial], *The News*, June 30, 1999.

not the language any country would use to indicate support for our position.[9]

Apart from the at best neutral posture adopted by China, Beijing's overtures to India were particularly vexing. Some writers sought to legitimize this Chinese peace gambit with such pithy statements as, "A big mountain can accommodate two tigers."[10]

By the end of July 1999, after the simultaneously much-lauded and much-loathed Sharif-Clinton joint statement, there was a consensus that Pakistan was diplomatically isolated and marginalized by even its closest allies. By mid-July, as will be discussed further in Chapter Three, there was an emergence of popular discontent with the Pakistani government's failure to predict both the international community's response to Pakistan's role in Kargil and India's reaction to what it perceived as an act of war.[11]

This accumulating international isolation and opprobrium, among other strategic and tactical concerns, likely precipitated Pakistan's decision to withdraw from Kashmir. While it seems reasonable to posit that China's response may have initiated disquiet about the durability of the expected or implied commitments presumed to inhere in Sino-Pakistan relations, senior officers in the Pakistani Army, the political leadership, and high-level civil servants suggested that they did not anticipate wide swings in their bilateral dealings with China.

This international isolation also impressed upon Pakistan the need to be seen as pursuing peace with India to recoup some of the diplomatic cachet it had in the immediate aftermath of India's nuclear tests. Pakistan's actions in this regard are difficult at best to interpret. On the one hand, Pakistan seems to understand that India has received high dividends from both its mastery of the rhetoric of restraint and its decision not to cross the LOC during the Kargil conflict. As a result, Pakistan has begun to appreciate that it needs to

---

[9]Abbas Rashid, "Raising the Ante in Kashmir."

[10]Afzal Mahmood, "Ties with China in Perspective."

[11]Afzal Mahmood, "Seeing Kargil in Perspective," *The Dawn*, July 18, 1999; M.B. Naqvi, "Looking Beyond Kargil," *The Dawn*, July 19, 1999; Lt. Gen. (Retd) Asad Durrani, "Beyond Kargil," *The News International Pakistan*, July 9, 1999.

cultivate the public persona of peace mongering. Indeed, in December 2000, Pakistan made several overt gestures toward pursuing peace. For example, Pakistan's current foreign minister, Abdul Sattar, offered India a trilateral process to commence before December 27, 2000, when the Indian-called Ramazan cease-fire was initially scheduled to conclude.[12] Pakistan has followed through with offers of maximum restraint, withdrawal from the LOC, and offers of talks at any time, level, or place. Pakistan also claims that it is trying to crack down on "jihadi elements," perhaps to counter India's much-aired exasperation with Pakistan's entrenched unwillingness to do so.[13] Pakistan's January 2001 airlift of aid to earthquake victims in India may also be read as an overt effort to reposition itself as a peace broker in the subcontinent.[14] Indeed, General Pervez Musharraf himself is trying to recast his image as "the mastermind of Kargil" to the one who solves the Kashmir conundrum.[15]

A straightforward analysis of Pakistan's strategy in this peace offensive is complicated by the gap between what Pakistan claims it has done and what Pakistan has verifiably done. One possible interpretation is that Pakistan is simply deploying the rhetoric of peace to regain international standing. There is some evidence to support this interpretation. For example, despite the proclamation of troop withdrawal from the LOC, there is no evidence that any thinning of Pakistan's peacetime deployments had actually occurred as of March 2000. Pakistan's claims to rein in the jihadis are even more dubious. Musharraf's much-heralded efforts to restrict the fund-collecting activities of jihadi *tanzeems* (organizations that support the jihadi efforts in Kashmir and elsewhere) have not been upheld by the Lahore High Court.[16] Moreover, the February 2001 controversy with *The*

---

[12]B. Muralidhar Reddy, "Sattar Wants Tripartite Talks Before Ramzan," *The Hindu*, December 5, 2000.

[13]B. Muralidhar Reddy, "Pak Vows Tough Measures Against 'Jihadi' Outfits," *The Hindu*, February 13, 2001; "Pakistan Vows Tough Action Against Extremists," *The Times of India Online*, February 13, 2001.

[14]K.J.M. Varma, "Pakistan to Airlift Tents, Blankets for Gujarat Quake Victims," rediff.com, January 29, 2001.

[15]"It's My Dream to Resolve Kashmir Issue: Musharraf," *The Times of India Online*, February 10, 2001.

[16]"Jihadis Cannot Be Stopped from Collecting Fund [sic]: Court," *The Times of India Online*, February 22, 2001.

Frontier Post illuminates Musharraf's inefficacy against Islamist elements.[17] His lack of will here does not simply reflect inability; rather, it reflects the deep ambivalence that many elites feel about the utility of the jihadis in Pakistan's overarching strategy. Surely, if Pakistan wants to meaningfully contribute to the peace process, it must make some very difficult decisions, the benefits of which are not yet uniformly clear to many Pakistani elites and to Pakistan's security managers.

Another possible interpretation of Pakistan's behavior in late 2000 and early 2001 is that Islamabad is engaged in some sort of tacit bargaining. This explanation is supported by the fact that Pakistan did reduce the number of infiltrations across the border in November and December 2000 after its offer of maximum restraint.[18] Pakistan appears to be trying to signal to India through this effort that it *can* rein in the jihadis and contribute to resolving Kashmir, conditioned on receiving the right—reciprocal—signals from New Delhi. Unfortunately, the unclassified evidence does not permit any easy evaluation of these competing interpretative frameworks.

The Scale of Operations

Two notions of "scale of operations" emerged during this analysis. One was the scale of Pakistani efforts in the conflict, and the other was the scale of India's reaction. As with the international response, the impact of these two notions of scale was deeply perspectival and depended greatly upon how knowledgeable the interlocutor was of Pakistan's true role in the crisis.

Those informants who knew of Pakistan's role believed that one important difference between Kargil and Pakistan's other activities was

---

[17]Barry Bearak, "Pakistani Journalists May Face Death for Publishing Letter," *New York Times*, February 19, 2001. *The Frontier Post* accidentally published an editorial that was considered blasphemous. The publication of the editorial precipitated an outcry for the editors' executions. In the face of this situation, Musharraf offered only weak statements, illuminating his lack of resolve against the jihadis and other extremist conservatives.

[18]See "Army Chief for Extension of Truce Beyond R-Day," *The Hindustan Times*, January 12, 2001. A competing hypothesis is that reduced infiltration could be ascribed to weather.

simply the scale and scope of the Pakistani operation. Retired high-level army officers, elements of the political leadership, academics, and think-tank analysts expressed this view. Generally, these individuals were not surprised that the Indians would respond in a rapid and decisive fashion. These informants were surprised, however, that Pakistan's security managers apparently did not have this expectation.

Those informants who did not know of Pakistan's role (or chose not to reveal such knowledge) generally expressed deep shock and indignation at India's aggressive response to the incursion.[19] These sentiments appear throughout the English coverage of the conflict. India's use of air power precipitated much bitterness, perhaps because India had not exercised this option since the 1971 war. An editorial from early June exemplifies this response to India's use of air power:

> The military operations in occupied Kashmir have been continuing for more than a decade now; and there is nothing new about them. If at all there is anything new, it lies in the level of force. . . .Never before, for instance, had India used its air force to prop up the sagging morale of its occupation forces. . . .Not content with that, the Indian military has stepped up its artillery bombardment . . . and even attempted small-scale infantry attacks across the Line of Control.[20]

It is important to note that this surprise seems to have stemmed from the belief that India was using unnecessary force against the mujahideen.[21] And in this vein, throughout May, June, and most of July, writers tended to portray Pakistan as aggrieved by what was seen as unjustifiable, naked Indian aggression against a handful of mujahideen. It is an unanswerable question whether these writers would have had the same opinion if they had known that the Pakistani Army was involved. Some evidence pointing to an affirmative

---

[19]Indeed, between June 1 and August 1, 1999, there were some 43 articles in *The Dawn* that addressed the issue of culpability for the escalation. Twenty-three of those articles clearly held the Indians responsible, compared to 10 articles that were more even-handed in their assessment.

[20]"Talks at Last" [editorial], *The Dawn*, June 10, 1999.

[21]Afzal Mahmood, "Defusing the Tension," *The Dawn*, June 5, 1999.

answer to this question is provided by the opinion pieces emerging in mid-July that asked why the Pakistani government misled the populace on Kargil. This shift in thought dampened the outrage over what was perceived to be Indian overreaction.[22]

The Possibility of Conflict Expansion

The final point of significance with respect to Pakistan is that many writers in Pakistan expressed numerous concerns about the possibility of the conflict's expansion into an all-out conventional war, which could further slip into a nuclear exchange.[23] Indeed, the Kargil crisis, having unfolded in the wake of the May 1998 nuclear tests by both combatants, may have been the most salient opportunity to reflect upon this possibility. However, some Indian observers were rather cynical about this Pakistani concern, feeling that this was simply a disingenuous Pakistani attempt, first, to generate anxiety about the nuclear issue in the international community and, second, to bolster Pakistan's efforts to precipitate international mediation in the Kashmir dispute.[24] While Pakistan's desire to raise the profile of the Kashmir issue has been an enduring component of its conventional and nuclear strategies, the *Kargil Review Committee Report* in this instance may be overstating the argument. A careful review of the chronology of Pakistan's ambiguous threats to use its "ultimate" weapons suggests that these warnings were issued only after India's conventional redeployments had reached significant proportions and were increasingly visible to Pakistani military intelligence. Under such circumstances, Islamabad's nuclear signaling is likely to have been driven, at least partly, by the prudential objective of cautioning New Delhi against any further escalation, vertical or horizontal, in its conventional military response along the international border.

---

[22]Dr. Manzur Ejaz, "An Unlikely Beneficiary of the Kargil Crisis."

[23]See, for example, "Defusing the Crisis" [editorial], *The Dawn*, June 5, 1999; "Before It Gets Any Worse" [editorial], *The Dawn*, May 27, 1999; "Playing with Fire" [editorial], *The Dawn*, May 30, 1999; Abdul Sattar, "Crisis with Deep Roots," *The News International Pakistan,* June 13, 1999; Shafqaat Mahmood (Senate Member), "Losing the Peace," *The News International Pakistan,* July 10, 1999.

[24]See, for example, India Kargil Review Committee, *From Surprise to Reckoning: The Kargil Review Committee Report* (New Delhi: Sage Publications, 2000), herefoth referred to in text as the *Kargil Review Committee Report.*

INDIA'S PERSPECTIVE

India Confirms Its Worst Beliefs About Pakistan

From India's perspective, the most significant conclusion drawn from Kargil is that dealing with Pakistan—as currently constituted—is going to be deeply problematic and perhaps even justifies minimal contact with Islamabad. This was the view expressed by a wide array of political leaders, analysts, and military officials in India, for several reasons.

First, Kargil demonstrated to India that Pakistan could be a reckless, adventuristic, and risk-acceptant state, capable of behaving astrategically and irrationally. Although surprised both by the fact and the intensity of the Kargil operation, almost all Indian analysts argued that—in retrospect—India ought not to have been surprised, because this event comported perfectly with the history of Pakistani adventurism witnessed specifically in 1947, and thereafter in 1964 and in 1965. For many interlocutors, particularly within the Indian government, this raised grave, usually unsettling questions about Pakistan's ability to assess its strategic environment, its capacity for coherent decisionmaking, and its ability to subordinate its fear and loathing of India to the more rational demands imposed by the nuclearization of the subcontinent and the fact of India's greater power-political capacity.

Second, Pakistan's prosecution of Kargil even amidst its pursuit of the Lahore Declaration process was understood to be outrageously duplicitous, irrespective of the strategic calculus—or lack thereof—motivating the operation. This view strengthens the argument within India that New Delhi really cannot "do business" with Islamabad because it is an essentially untrustworthy partner. It also reinforces Indian convictions that the international community cannot be allowed to railroad India into consummating some kind of a "peace process" with Pakistan, given the past failures of both Shimla and Lahore. More significantly, however, the "duplicity" of Pakistan, made evident by the Kargil adventure, is seen throughout the Indian government to necessitate critical changes in attitudes, institutions, capabilities, and readiness in order to deal with future Pakistani surprises in both the conventional military and the nuclear realms.

Third, Pakistan's chronic civil-military rivalry exacerbates India's distrust and wariness of the state. The Pakistani Army is and will likely remain the vaunted power in Pakistan, even when under a nominally civilian government. This institution is seen in New Delhi as being virulently anti-India. Given this perception, the fact of Kargil and the sketchy details available in India about the operation's genesis, planning, and execution only confirm the Indian suspicion that no matter what improvements in relations can be envisaged as occurring with Pakistan's civilian governments, these improvements will either be held hostage by the Pakistani military or will not be brought to consummation because of military opposition within Pakistan. This problem in turn leads Indian policymakers not only to despair of reaching any viable agreements with Pakistan, but also to avoid expending inordinate amounts of political capital to reach meaningful agreements because of (a) Islamabad's inability to recognize that the problem of "Kashmir" as defined by Pakistan cannot be enthroned as the "core" problem bedeviling India-Pakistan relations; (b) the Indian fears that even valid agreements reached with Pakistan will not stick or will be diluted by Islamabad depending on the political exigencies of the day; and (c) the concerns in New Delhi that even advantageous agreements reached with Islamabad could strengthen the Pakistani military and reinforce its propensity to continue warring with India.[25] In some sense, then, Indian policymakers and security managers believe that the Pakistani Army is the root of all major problems between India and Pakistan. Colonel Gurmeet Kanwal captured this sentiment exactly when he argued that

> India's problems in Kashmir will remain until Pakistan's rogue army is tamed. . . .The real problem between India and Pakistan is the Pakistan army and its abnormal influence in Pakistan's affairs, and not Kashmir or any other issue. Till democracy takes root in Pakistan, Indo-Pak problems will remain irreconcilable.[26]

---

[25]Many policymakers in New Delhi noted that this issue undercuts India's willingness to conclude satisfactory deals with Pakistan—for example, with respect to oil pipelines running over Pakistani territory or with respect to trade.

[26]Gurmeet Kanwal, "Nawaz Sharif's Damning Disclosures," *The Pioneer*, August 16, 2000.

India Strengthened in Its Determination to Marginalize Pakistan on Kashmir

While all but the most fringe elements recognize that the Kashmiri uprising in 1989 had indigenous roots, Indian stakeholders and the polity at large have been divided on the reasons for its longevity. Many have asserted that there is widespread alienation among the Kashmiris that must be addressed before the Kashmir issue can be resolved. This alienation is posited to stem from, inter alia, the poor human rights situation, problems with structures of popular representation, the lack of accountable state government, the persistence of center-state conflicts, and hardships imposed by counterinsurgency operations.[27] Others have taken the position that Pakistan is essentially the only obstacle to the Kashmiris finding a livable solution within India. Within these broad positions, some people have held that there is value in engaging the Pakistanis on Kashmir for the purposes of moderating and attenuating Pakistan's activities. The Lahore Declaration can be seen in this light.

In India's view, the Lahore initiative was a legitimate (and, for Vajpayee himself, a determined) effort to achieve normalization on a broad cluster of key issues.[28] Kargil, likely launched around the time of the Lahore initiative, raised serious doubts about India's ability to deal with Pakistan in good faith. Well-placed interlocutors in the Prime Minister's Office, Ministry of Defense, and Ministry of External Affairs explained that one of the most important changes in the Indian mindset precipitated by Kargil is that those who formerly were proponents of engaging Pakistan have been silenced or no longer support this position. Even those on the left of the political spectrum who formerly contended that diplomacy was a critical component of resolving the Kashmir problem now opine that Pakistan cannot be trusted, and almost all political constituencies in India are united in the belief that negotiations—as opposed to merely "talks"—are not an option now or in the future. The distinction between negotiations and talks is an important one: whereas the latter involves, among

---

[27]Sumantra Bose, "Kashmir: Sources of Conflict, Dimensions of Peace," *Survival*, Vol. 41, No. 3, Autumn 1999, pp. 149–171.

[28]See the text of the Lahore Declaration, which can be obtained from the U.S. Institute of Peace Web site: http://www.usip.org/library/pa/ip/ip_lahore19990221. html.

other things, procedural and diplomatic engagement, the former involves some prospect of substantive concessions. While India has
time and again affirmed its willingness to engage *procedurally and
diplomatically* with Pakistan, its incentives to engage in negotiations
that harbor the prospect of *substantive* concessions of the sort desired by Pakistan—a plebiscite in accordance with the UN resolutions, a redrawing of the territorial boundaries to include a possible
transfer of the Kashmir valley to Pakistan, or a trifurcation of the
state of Jammu and Kashmir along religious-ethnic lines—have always been minimal. This calculus has only been reinforced by the
events occurring at Kargil.

All this implies that the motivation to treat Pakistan as a legitimate
party to the Kashmir dispute in the sense traditionally understood by
Islamabad—which was never very significant to begin with—is now
all but extinguished, and New Delhi will pursue, as best it can, solutions to the Kashmir problem that either bypass or marginalize Pakistan in the substantive (though not the procedural) sense. Any Pakistani engagement on the question of Kashmir is likely to be mainly
supplemental to internal Indian efforts at restoring local peace.

Kargil Was an Intelligence Failure Not to Be Repeated

Kargil was a significant blow to India's perception of its security.
Media reports, interviews with key military and political individuals,
and numerous monographs written to assess the causes and outcomes of the Kargil debacle all conclude that Pakistan's adventurism
in Kargil was a tactical and strategic surprise.[29] Several high-level
military and political stakeholders in India have described Kargil as
India's Pearl Harbor, which has compelled New Delhi to take various
steps to ensure that a similar situation will not occur.

The significance of the strategic surprise is manifested in at least two
ways. The first is that the Indian political-military elite has begun to
identify the limitations that exist in Indian intelligence's ability to
collect, analyze, and disseminate intelligence effectively. Accus-

---

[29]The primary public document that addresses this issue is the India Kargil Review
Committee's *From Surprise to Reckoning: The Kargil Review Committee Report*. This
document covers the shortfalls of Indian intelligence equipment and the inherent
deficiencies of the Indian intelligence apparatus.

tomed to a seasonal pattern of summer diligence followed by a winter of recuperative retreat, the Indian military and their attendant intelligence agencies did little to anticipate a Pakistani foray into LOC locations typically held by India. The intelligence agencies were described as relying too heavily on the notion that the inhospitable region and the lack of previous Pakistani adventurism precluded any type of incursion into Kargil.[30]

Second, the *Kargil Review Committee Report* makes clear that there were serious lapses in what can be considered baseline intelligence collection. For instance, the Research & Analysis Wing (R&AW) failed to correctly identify as many as five infantry battalions of the Pakistani Northern Light Infantry (NLI) and the de-induction of three others.[31] Opinion pieces in newspapers following evidence of strategic surprise were equally critical of the intelligence failure. An especially harsh rebuke of the Indian Army represents the most debasing public response to the intelligence failure:

> [H]ow did these posts get occupied by the infiltrators? This constant shelling should have been taken as an ominous sign. I am afraid we were not prepared. The euphoria since May 1998 has lulled our politicians and public alike. But as a former military intelligence chief, I would not spare the army too. When you are holding posts at those heights and are in eyeball-to-eyeball contact with the adversary, not being able to see their movements, leave alone anticipate them, is inexcusable. It is certainly an intelligence failure.[32]

The timing of the incursion, the diplomatic context in which it occurred, and Pakistan's tactical audacity occasioned much introspection among India's military, political, and intelligence officials. Kargil precipitated a renewed dedication to military, technological, and intelligence efforts to preclude future Kargil-like scenarios. This issue is further addressed in Chapter Three, which discusses lessons learned from Kargil.

---

[30]Ibid., p. 160.

[31]Ibid., p. 153.

[32]Lt. Gen. K.S. Khajuria, "Kargil Task Not an Easy One," *The Times of India,* May 29, 1999.

India Realizes That International Attention to Pakistani Adventurism Can Be Positive

The various statements made by the international community were highly sympathetic to India's position during the Kargil crisis, a condition that India appreciated. A reading of the Indian op-ed pages of major English-language papers suggests that India may have concluded that select types of international attention can be beneficial in some contexts, particularly when focused on Pakistani misdeeds.

The international response to Kargil nearly unanimously cast Pakistan as the transgressor and called for mutual restraint, a bilateral settlement of disputes, and a resumption of the Lahore process—all of which supported India's position on Kashmir generally and Kargil in particular. As noted above, even China espoused a rhetoric that was consonant with the measured international response.[33] For example, the Chinese foreign ministry spokesman, Zhu Bangzao, explained: "China hopes India and Pakistan will exercise restraint and peacefully resolve their differences and problems through patient and sincere dialogue."[34]

Conversely, India both maintained the support of old friends and cultivated new bastions of support. Russia, for example, was "the first country to come out openly in support of India by a categorical declaration that it would foil Pakistan's bid to internationalise the Kashmir issue whilst reiterating its support for New Delhi's action against the infiltrators in Kargil."[35] (Russia may have been motivated to take such a position because of its own situation in Chechnya.) Given the long history of estrangement between the United States and India and the intense U.S. pressure on New Delhi in relation to

---

[33]K. K. Katyal, "Pak Wooing China," *The Hindu,* June 10, 1999; C. Raja Mohan, "China Unlikely to Adopt Anti-India Posture," *The Hindu,* June 11, 1999.

[34]"Show Restraint: China," *The Pioneer,* May 28, 1999; "Resume Talks, China Tells Sharif," *The Hindu,* June 29, 1999; and "Kashmir Is Not Kosovo," *The Pioneer,* May 30, 1999.

[35]Arpit Rajain, "India's Political and Diplomatic Response to the Kargil Crisis," unpublished working paper, p. 8. See also "Kargil Infiltrators Are Fundamentalists: Russia," *The Hindustan Times,* May 29, 1999; Vladimir Radyuhin, "Moscow Backs Operation Against Intruders," *The Hindu,* May 28, 1999; "Assurance from Russia" [editorial], *The Hindustan Times,* May 30, 1999.

its nuclear programs, India was particularly surprised by the U.S. reaction to the events in Kargil, which insinuated the Pakistani role in the crisis by insisting upon Pakistan's withdrawal of the combatants.[36] Moreover, the United States countered the notion that Pakistan was provoked into retaliating against what it was trying to paint as clear Indian aggression by stating that "to our knowledge, India has not struck over the Line of Control, deliberately or accidentally."[37] The U.S. State Department was also quoted as saying that sanctions might be imposed against Pakistan if it continued with its intransigent posture.[38] Additionally, India received accolades for acting with restraint in the face of naked Pakistani aggression.[39] It may even be suggested that Kargil catalyzed a major shift in U.S. policy away from its traditional formula, which affirms Kashmir as a dispute to be resolved by India and Pakistan, toward a position effectively recognizing the sanctity of the LOC, a development that is welcomed by New Delhi.

The response from multilateral organizations was also viewed by Indian elites as favorable. The United Nations, particularly members of the Security Council, assured India there would be no attempt to intervene in Kashmir, although Pakistan was said to have requested such intervention.[40] Rather, the UN would maintain its position of observer along the LOC.[41] Similarly, the G-8 issued a statement on June 21, 1999, indicating its "deep concern" about the military confrontation in Kashmir, which it saw as being the result of an "infiltration of armed intruders which violated the line of control."[42]

---

[36]See the July 4 Clinton-Sharif Agreement. See also Sridhar Krishnaswami, "Pull Back Forces, Clinton Tells Sharif," *The Hindu*, June 16, 1999.

[37]"U.S. Rejects Pak Claims on LOC Violations," *The Times of India*, May 28, 1999.

[38]Sridhar Krishnaswami, "Zinni Mission to Pak, Very Productive," *The Hindu*, June 29, 1999. See also C. Raja Mohan, "Will U.S. Match Words with Deeds?" *The Hindu*, June 26, 1999; Amit Baruah, "U.S. Asks Pak to Pull Out Intruders," *The Hindu*, June 25, 1999.

[39]See, for example, "Clinton Appreciates India's Restraint," *The Hindu*, June 15, 1999.

[40]Amit Baruah, "Pakistan Wants International Attention," *The Hindu*, May 28, 1999.

[41]For more discussion regarding the UN reaction to events in Kargil, see Arpit Rajain, "India's Political and Diplomatic Response to the Kargil Crisis." See also "Security Council Hands Off Kargil," *The Statesman*, May 30, 1999; "Pakistan Crossed the LOC Says UN Chief," *The Hindu*, May 31, 1999.

[42]"G-8 Communiqué," June 1999. See also "G-8 Can Now Play Proactive Role in Indo-Pak Conflict," *The Hindustan Times Online Edition*, June 22, 1999.

The communiqué called for a "restoration of the line of control and for the parties to work for an immediate cessation of the fighting, full respect in the future for the line of control and the resumption of the dialogue between India and Pakistan in the spirit of the Lahore Declaration." The language of the communiqué was clearly consistent with the Indian interest in legitimizing the LOC as a border between the two nations based on a bilateral agreement.

The international reaction to the Kargil intrusion, particularly from the United States, G-8, UN, and China, demonstrated to India the power of world opinion to restrict Pakistan's options at all levels of diplomacy and war. The *Kargil Review Committee Report* suggested that India was cognizant of the role that international perception played in the unraveling of Kargil and would seek to develop and exploit that perception.[43] To the degree that Pakistani support for pariah regimes like the Taliban remains unwavering and to the degree that Islamist radicalism extends its reach beyond Kashmir, India's location as a front-line state in the fight against political extremism will be all the more obvious.[44] India has thus learned to value international attention to Pakistani adventurism, but it should not therefore be concluded that India sees benefit accruing from internationalizing the Kashmir issue more generally. On the contrary, India will persist in its efforts to minimize the role of other countries and international organizations in any discussions regarding the disposition of Kashmir even while it cultivates attention that has the effect of demonizing and ultimately constraining Pakistan.

Kargil Demonstrated the Utility of the Media in Military Operations

The *Kargil Review Committee Report* states that

> The media is or can be a valuable force multiplier. Even in circumstances of proxy war, the battle for hearts and minds is of

---

[43]See, for instance, "Pakistan's Dilemma," *The Hindustan Times*, June 30, 1999. See also "The Line of Crisis," *The Indian Express*, June 29, 1999; "Taming Pakistan," *The Times of India*, June 26, 1999; "Pakistan's Plan Backfires," *The Pioneer*, June 25, 1999; "India and the U.S. After Kargil," *The Hindu*, June 24, 1999.

[44]India Kargil Review Committee, *From Surprise to Reckoning: The Kargil Review Committee Report*, p. 222.

paramount importance. It is little use winning the battle of bullets only to lose the war because of popular alienation.[45]

A review of Indian military literature suggests that India has long been aware of the need to develop a media strategy as an instrument of warfare. The need for such a strategy has been reinforced by India's extensive involvement in counterinsurgency (COIN) and peacekeeping operations.[46] During Kargil, New Delhi demonstrated its agility in handling a variety of media (e.g., television, print, radio, Internet) to disseminate and control the Indian message, shaping in the process both the international and the domestic perception of events.

The role of the media in shaping domestic and international opinion regarding Kargil is evident in the headlines of major Indian newspapers printed during the time. Numerous Indian newspapers were filled with accounts of how Pakistan "propped up intruders" in a "qualitatively different" infiltration. Such narratives in effect strengthened the view of India as a responsible and restrained nuclear nation victimized by its overzealous neighbor. Some representative headlines are as follows:

"Evidence of Pak Intruders on Indian Side," *The Hindu*, May 29, 1999.

"Intrusion Obviously Had Full Backing of Pak Government: India," *The Hindustan Times*, May 27, 1999.

"Pakistan Army Officers Among Kargil Infiltrators," *The Statesman*, May 25, 1999.

---

[45]Ibid., p. 215.

[46]Maj. Gen. Arjun Ray, *Kashmir Diary: Psychology of Militancy* (New Delhi: Manas Publications, 1997). Also see Pegasus, "Insurgency and Counter-Insurgency: The Anatomy of an Insurgent Movement and Counter Measures," *Indian Defence Review*, Vol. 1, No. 1, January 1996; Lt. Gen. Vijay Madan, "Population Terrain—The Neglected Factor of Counter-Insurgency Operations," *Indian Defence Review*, Vol. 12, No. 2, April–June, 1997; Col. D. P. Merchant, "Peacekeeping in Somalia: An Indian Experience," *Army & Defence Quarterly Journal*, Vol. 126, April 1996, pp. 134–141.

Headlines such as these focused attention on a "blitz" of stories that "expose[d] the direct role of Pakistan" in the invasion of Indian territory.[47]

Various print and television stories also painted India as a nation at the front line of Islamic terrorism. The Indian press made explicit references to the connection between Pakistan and vilified Afghanistan resident Osama bin Laden.[48] Such overtures were perhaps symptomatic of India's efforts to stimulate antipathy toward its unstable, nonsecular neighbor. Conversely, at an early stage in the conflict, India sought to cast itself in an aura of responsibility and trust.[49] By publicly disavowing crossing the LOC—despite enormous provocation from Pakistan—India cultivated an international opinion that it was a responsible nuclear nation capable of restraint.

Another important objective in the aftermath of Kargil was the ex post facto recasting of India's engagement with Pakistan during the Lahore Declaration process. Early in the crisis, the Indian media rushed to proclaim Pakistani Prime Minister Nawaz Sharif's ignorance of Kargil and cast him as the Pakistani Army's duped stooge. Assuming ignorance was not at issue—an assumption that cannot be taken for granted to begin with—this image had utility for two reasons. First, it was a "carefully calculated move to sharpen the differences between civilian and military establishments in Pakistan."[50] Second, by casting the Pakistani Army as the rogue elephant responsible for Kargil and by distancing the Sharif government from it, India could insist that the Lahore Declaration represented a legitimate form of engagement that was being subverted principally by the Pakistani Army—a strategy that had some attractiveness insofar as it

---

[47]"Delhi Plans Publicity Blitz to Expose Direct Role of Pakistan," *The Hindustan Times,* May 30, 1999.

[48]"Kargil Infiltrators Are Fundamentalists: Russia"; B. Raman, "Is Osama bin Laden in Kargil?" *The Indian Express,* May 26, 1999; "Taliban Are Waiting to Launch Jehad in Kashmir," *The Asian Age,* June 16, 1999; "German Intelligence Says Osama Is Involved in the Kashmir Crisis," *The Asian Age,* June 16, 1999.

[49]Arpit Rajain, "India's Political and Diplomatic Response to the Kargil Crisis."

[50]Ibid.

could help vitiate the claims of some of the critics of Vajpayee's dramatic bus diplomacy.[51]

One of the positive benefits of the media's televised depiction of India's war dead was the galvanizing of domestic support for more-aggressive actions against Pakistan.[52] This was watched with interest in Pakistan, according to our interlocutors, who read these depictions as a deliberate effort to instigate a frenzied consensus in favor of attacking Pakistan. Indian media agencies also cultivated domestic support with continuous news of activities on the front lines and instant communication via the Internet. Several Web sites (e.g., www.indiainfo.com, www.kargilonline.com, and www.vijayinkargil. org) described numerous episodes of heroism at the front, supported Indian tactical and strategic decisions, updated events in real time, and narrated stories of families of soldiers enduring the loss of their loved ones.

While these Web sites have obvious utility in some regards, the demographics of India imply that only a small fraction of India's more-affluent population was on-line and therefore accessible through this medium. It is also likely that these Web sites targeted the expatriate Indian population (which has developed considerable political clout within some countries of residence). Some of these Web sites explicitly solicited financial donations. For example, kargilonline.com (a site dedicated to the "welfare of soldiers and their families") tried to encourage donations to the Army Welfare Fund: "The debt of gratitude the nation owes these heroes is incalculable. Nevertheless, ordinary citizens like you and me must find some small way to chip in."[53] The Indian Army's official Kargil Web site (www.vijayinkargil. org) did so also: "Contributions [for the Army Welfare Fund] including those from the NRI's [nonresident Indians] are welcome (in any currency)."[54]

---

[51]Ibid. See also "Sharif, ISI Uninvolved, by George!" *The Hindustan Times,* May 29, 1999; "Nawas Was Bypassed, Feel Western Experts," *The Pioneer,* May 29, 1999.

[52]See "Pak Sends Mutilated Bodies Ahead of Aziz," *Indian Express,* June 11, 1999; "Pak Ploy to Escalate War, Draw Global Attention," *The Pioneer,* June 11, 1999; John Wilson, "Enough. Now Teach Them a Lesson," *The Pioneer,* June 11, 1999.

[53]www.kargilonline.com.

[54]www.vijayinkargil.org.

The mobilization of national and international opinion in support of India is seen as a key component of future conflicts with Pakistan. In fact, the *Kargil Review Committee Report* recommends a well-structured civil-military apparatus to ensure all possible media consistently and adequately portray the desired Indian message.[55] The significance of incorporating a comprehensive information warfare component—one that is completely integrated with national reportage capabilities—cannot be overstated. Both the declared desire to improve civil-military relations in order to mold positive perceptions among the domestic audience and the implied intention to ensure India's posture of stability and restraint in the international realm are key pieces of evidence that words are viewed as carrying great weight in the ongoing battle for hearts and minds in the subcontinent and beyond.

SUMMARY

The import of the Kargil crisis was generally very different for both countries. While Pakistan appears to have concluded that Kargil-like operations are not likely to be successful for many reasons and therefore are not attractive as a matter of state policy, Pakistan has *not* concluded that violence in general is an illegitimate means for altering the status quo. Pakistan will continue to pursue low-intensity operations within the context of its Kashmir policy, incorporating as best it can ordinary Kashmiris' alienation from India in support of larger political objectives. One of the reasons why future Kargil-like episodes are seen as not likely to be successful is Pakistan's understanding that the conflict subverted Pakistan's position internationally while simultaneously retarding its ability to focus on economic and social renewal domestically.

What remains to be explicated is Pakistan's continual willingness to take on such risks. In fact, several Pakistani writers have questioned Pakistan's foray into Kargil, comparing it with the 1965 war as a fine

---

[55]India Kargil Review Committee, *From Surprise to Reckoning: The Kargil Review Committee Report*, pp. 214–219.

example of why Pakistan should resist such adventurism.[56] More generally, prior to launching this operation, Islamabad should well have comprehended India's ability to inflict pain on Pakistan. Pakistan's risk acceptance is revisited in the next chapter.

Most of Kargil's significance for India can be seen in terms of the conflict's impact on bilateral relations with Pakistan. India believes Pakistan to be fundamentally untrustworthy and capable of acting in ways that appear to be completely irrational and astrategic. This has strengthened the Indian determination to resolve the Kashmir issue without acknowledging Pakistan's equities in the manner desired by Islamabad. Kargil also occasioned reconsideration of India's perception of its security and its intelligence apparatus: in particular, Kargil strengthened the belief that Pakistani surprises can and will occur with potentially dangerous results and that they consequently merit anticipatory preparation in India. Kargil also revealed to India that select aspects of international attention—particularly to Pakistan's misconduct—have significant utility for its grand strategy. Finally, Kargil demonstrated India's ability to dexterously influence the media to shape the domestic and the international response.

---

[56]M. B. Naqvi, "Looking Beyond Kargil"; Gen-Maj. (Retd) M. Akbar, "Time for Sober Reflection," *The Dawn*, July 22, 1999; Shahid M. Amin, "Kargil: The Unanswered Questions II—Time to Shed Illusions," *The Dawn*, July 26, 1999.

Chapter Three

KARGIL: LESSONS LEARNED ON BOTH SIDES

Our analysis elicited very different lessons learned for India and Pakistan. In the case of Pakistan, most of the lessons learned are strategic rather than operational or tactical in the military sense. This is in part because the open-source reporting of the operation generally denied the presence of Pakistani regulars, which necessarily precluded any open discussion of war-fighting lessons learned.[1] Generally, Pakistan does not have a rich tradition of open accounts of its military operations, which stands in some contrast to India's more robust private—though not official—publishing industry on political-military affairs.

For Pakistan, the apparent lessons learned from Kargil are principally as follows:

- Pakistan now views Kargil-like operations as an ineffective means of dispute resolution—mainly because Kargil appears to have been such a failure in the eyes of the world. The significance of this conclusion, however, is limited by the fact that many stakeholders in Pakistan *simultaneously* believe that Kargil can be seen as a victory of sorts. This continuing ambiguity about the effect of Kargil, when coupled with the strong Pakistani belief in the utility of other kinds of coercive operations against India, has unsettling consequences for the prospect of lasting stability.

---

[1]In general, open-source reporting that alleged direct involvement of the Pakistani Army began to emerge only well after the crisis ended. One excellent example is M. Ilyas Khan, "Life After Kargil," *The Herald*, July 2000, pp. 24–30.

- To preclude strategic failure of the kind represented by Kargil in the future, Pakistan must effectively appraise the international response and the operational implications of that response. In particular, Pakistan must better assess the reactions of its adversaries in furtherance of a more effective grand strategy.

- Pakistan needs a broad body of experts, perhaps like the National Security Council (NSC), to adequately assess its planned operations of this sort. This sentiment is aroused by the government's sweeping failure to anticipate the sequelae of the Kargil crisis and the secrecy in which the operation was shrouded. This veil of secrecy is the manifestation of the deep fissures in Pakistan's civil-military relations.

- Pakistan must develop specific media strategies to shape international opinion and to mitigate India's advantages on the information battleground. However, even the best media strategy cannot provide insulation against duplicity in the long term. Recognizing this problem, some interlocutors suggested that Pakistan made a grave miscalculation by hiding behind the transparent mujahideen cover story.

- Because the use of Pakistani regulars in Kargil proved to be counterproductive and because Pakistan believes that it has few or no diplomatic options, Pakistan sees only one successful strategy for bringing India to the negotiating table: the continued prosecution of subconventional conflict in Kashmir and perhaps elsewhere in India.

- Pakistan's nuclear capabilities have become the key to successful execution of its political strategies at multiple levels. Nuclear weapons not only enable Islamabad to pursue "strategic diversion" and immunize the country from a violent Indian counterresponse, they also serve to catalyze the attention and, Pakistan hopes, the interest of the international community. Consequently, they have acquired centrality in Pakistan's national strategy.

In stark contrast to Pakistan's guarded and even deceptive accounts of Kargil, India has been very critical of key operational areas and has published several accounts of the operation, though none are as yet either complete or definitive.[2]   The principal lessons that India learned from Kargil are as follows:

- India must be prepared for Pakistani recklessness, which could occur in different areas and take different forms: terrorism throughout India, conventional operations and incursions, increased LIC in Kashmir, and a variety of nontraditional threats.

- India must more aggressively counter Pakistani threats along the LOC by investing in more technologically advanced military and intelligence equipment. India is considering a complete overhaul of its intelligence infrastructure in light of its embarrassing failure to identify the Pakistani infiltration. However, despite initial humiliations, India is now confident that it can effectively counter the most audacious conventional Pakistani threats along the LOC even when disadvantaged by surprise.

- The Kashmir issue cannot be neglected in hopes of gradual atrophy. Rather, its resolution requires high-level attention and commitment as well as creative responses on the part of the government.

- India understands that international support cannot be taken for granted. To ensure this support, India must both maintain a posture of responsibility and be seen as seeking peace. These requirements act as an important brake on India's propensity to respond aggressively to future Pakistani provocations.

- India recognizes the utility of the media in contemporary conflicts and will continue its offensive in the information war. India believes that it won Kargil politically in part because of its dexterous capability of shaping international perception. India also values the role of perception management in affecting public opinion domestically as well as influencing the morale of the Indian and Pakistani militaries.

---

[2]See, for example, India Kargil Review Committee, *From Surprise to Reckoning: The Kargil Review Committee Report*; Air Commodore Jasjit Singh, *Kargil 1999: Pakistan's Fourth War for Kashmir* (New Delhi: Knowledge World, 1999); Col. Ravi Nanda, *Kargil: A Wakeup Call* (New Delhi: Lancer Books, 1999); Col. Bhaskar Sarkar, *Kargil War: Past, Present and Future* (New Delhi: Lancer Publishers, 1999).

- India must treat nuclear issues more carefully because Pakistan is a risk-acceptant state capable of "irrational" strategic surprises. India thus must be prepared for nuclear operations that may be forced upon it by Pakistani actions.

The next two sections explicate these various lessons learned by the two combatants.

PAKISTAN'S PERSPECTIVE

Premeditated Kargil-like Operations Are Not an Effective Means of Dispute Resolution, But Kargil Itself May Not Have Been an Unmitigated "Failure"

Retired and uniformed military officers, the political leadership, foreign office bureaucrats, and opinion shapers and analysts widely agree that perhaps the most important lesson learned from Kargil is that such operations are not an effective means for advancing Pakistan's strategic interests and hence are likely to be a less-than-attractive strategy in the policy-relevant future. The reasons cited for this conclusion are numerous and include the following:

- India is not likely to provide the opportunity. India is making (or is likely to make) investments that would seriously hinder any future Kargil-like operations.

- The international community will not tolerate future attempts to change the status quo, so it is in Pakistan's best interests to avoid such operations.

- Kashmir is a political problem that requires a diplomatic rather than a military solution.

- Kargil was too costly in multiple ways, and Pakistan cannot gamble with such risks again.

- The failure of the operation itself is instructive and ought to be a deterrent to reconsidering such options in the future.

Several opinion shapers argue that in the face of such barriers to pursuing Kargil-like operations in the future, Pakistan will have to address its own political and economic weaknesses. For example, Shahid M. Amin, a career diplomat who has served the Pakistani Foreign Office in the capacity of ambassador for 18 years, articulated a commonly held opinion when he stated the following:

> It is high time that the country became ruthlessly realistic about its limitations and priorities. First and foremost, Pakistan's survival must precede everything else, *including our attachment to the Kashmir cause.* Secondly, it has to be understood that our economy is our weakest point and has to be given priority over any other consideration. Thirdly, we need to set our house in order and require a long period of internal consolidation, based on drastic reforms.[3] (Emphasis added.)

Aziz Siddiqui, formerly the editor and joint director of the Human Rights Commission of Pakistan (HRCP), asserted the failure of Kargil—and the failure of future Kargils—most clearly when he wrote:

> Can there be other ways [other than Kargil] to persuade India towards a reasonable approach in Kashmir? More Kargils may not do this. . . .[If] one action fails to prove persuasively, there should be little reason to believe that others of that kind will turn out much better. . . .[There is only one remaining] opportunity for Pakistan— which is somehow to create a demonstration effect that accommodation and good relations with it are in India's own best practical interest. That can happen only if Pakistan sets about concentrating almost exclusively on becoming a strong and stable political and economic entity in the region. . . .This is no doubt a longer-term process. But certainly not as long term as the fifty years we have spent trying to resolve Kashmir and making it even worse confounded with each try. It is also, after all, elementary common sense to discard the methods that have not worked, and which on all sound judgment look unlikely to work, and look for other ways.[4]

Numerous other writers and interlocutors reiterated the argument that future Kargil-like episodes are neither sustainable nor viable op-

---

[3]Shahid M. Amin, "Kargil: The Unanswered Questions II—Time to Shed Illusions."

[4]Aziz Siddiqui, "In the Aftermath of 'Jihad,'" *The Dawn,* July 11, 1999.

tions.[5] As one editorialist succinctly put it, "The strongest grantor [sic] of Kashmiri freedom is a strong Pakistan. This is a lesson of Kargil."[6]

This lesson of a strong Pakistan ought to be particularly attractive to Pakistan's armed services. One analyst pointed out that since General Musharraf is now Pakistan's Chief Executive, he has a much more significant understanding of the importance of the fiscal, political, and social health of his nation *and, most importantly, he is now directly responsible for these concerns.* One could conjecture that in his capacity as leader of Pakistan, Musharraf may understand the dividends that could accrue to Pakistan's development if he can sell a compromise on the Kashmir issue to the Pakistani polity (likely the conversion of the LOC, with some modification, into an international border), deal with Islamist extremism, and resolve bilateral problems with India. Yet Musharraf is likely leery of mustering the political will to accomplish these tasks because the political fallout of such a move could risk discrediting the institution of the Pakistani Army, a move that Musharraf, an Army officer, might be rather unwilling to take. (It would also run counter to the desire of some elements of the Pakistani military to continue "bleeding" India in Kashmir either as a form of preventive self-defense or as revenge for the debacle of 1971.) Thus, it may be preferable that a civilian government undertake these decisions to compromise—and shoulder the ensuing political consequences. Musharraf's predicament, according to many Pakistani analysts, embodies the tension between what needs to be done and what he can actually do, a point that will be revisited later in this report.

While there is obviously a significant body of opinion in Pakistan that Islamabad ought to look beyond Kashmir and focus on renewing Pakistan itself, the benefits of this judgment are often undermined by the existence of strong competing views that do not generally reject

---

[5]See "Kargil: Where Do We Go from Here" [letter to the editor], *The Dawn*, July 10, 1999; Abbas Rashid, "Raising the Ante in Kashmir"; Imtiaz Gul, "Retreat Dictated by Economic Compulsions," *The News International Pakistan*, July 10, 1999; Shafqaat Mahmood, "Losing the Peace"; Mahdi Masud, "Kargil Crisis: A Balance Sheet," *The Dawn*, July 16, 1999; Altaf Gauhar, "Four Wars, One Assumption," *The Nation*, September 5, 1999.

[6]"Prime Minister Explains" [editorial], *The Dawn*, July 14, 1999.

violence as a legitimate means of altering the status quo—a point that will be revisited later—and, more specifically, do not view the Kargil operation itself as an unmitigated failure. While vocal criticisms of the misadventure that was Kargil have been plentiful, it would be incorrect to conclude that various strata of the Pakistani leadership have not seen value from that operation. Even though there is wide consensus that Pakistan paid a heavy price for initiating the Kargil conflict, a large and significant number of uniformed and retired military officers, senior political leaders, and analysts *simultaneously* argue that Kargil can be read as a success in certain respects. There are several variants of this story, all of which together portend disturbing consequences for strategic stability.

One view that was commonly expressed by informants is that India's cease-fire offer, its willingness to let the All Parties Hurriyat Conference (APHC) go to Pakistan, and its successive extensions of the cease-fire in Kashmir arose because of Kargil. Kargil, it was argued, demonstrated to India that its Kashmir policy is costly and that Pakistan's LIC strategy is relatively inexpensive. Thus, many stakeholders within Pakistan attribute the extent to which India's peace overtures are legitimate to the fact of Kargil. To that degree at least, this viewpoint would hold, the Kargil operation—even if it besmirched Pakistan's reputation internationally—successfully contributed to Pakistan's strategic objectives vis-à-vis Kashmir.

A second common variant is that Kargil was a tactical success but a strategic failure. This view was also articulated by a number of informants and has been reiterated in various articles. Shireen Mazari, for example, has written that "the military aspect of the Kargil action was simply brilliant." Later in the same piece she laments that India was able to "turn a military defeat into a diplomatic victory . . . [and] that Pakistan was unable to translate a tremendous military success into a politico-diplomatic victory."[7] Interlocutors who held this view asserted—often against the weight of evidence—that the Pakistani Army's operational performance at Kargil was flawless, and they invariably concluded that the Army's attainment of strategic surprise at Kargil was in effect synonymous with the achievement of victory in

---

[7]Shireen M. Mazari, "Re-Examining Kargil," *Defence Journal* (online version), June 2000.

the campaign writ large. Since those who hold this view entirely ne-
glect the fact that the Indian Army, once mobilized, redeployed, and
committed to eviction operations, actually secured repeated tactical
victories—often against great odds—throughout the concluding half
of the Kargil campaign, they continue to claim that Kargil must be
chalked up as an operational victory for the Pakistani Army even if it
otherwise appears to be an unnecessary political defeat for Pakistan
at large.

A third and related narrative suggests that the Pakistani Army (or in
some treatments the "mujahideen") could have held out until the
winter snowfall, giving an honorable cover for retreat, had Prime
Minister Nawaz Sharif not sold them out in Washington during his
July 4 meeting with President Clinton. According to this argument,
Pakistan could have easily maintained its commanding operational-
tactical positions along the occupied hilltops while, more importantly, India was not in a position to widen the war. Shireen Mazari,
representing this view as well, has argued that "[t]he reality is that
there was simply no danger of even an all-out war between Pakistan
and India because India was not in a position to instigate such a
war."[8] While Mazari may be dismissed as one of the hawkish voices
of the fringe of Pakistan's security managers, other, less hawkish interlocutors made similar arguments. For example, one academic
analyst argued that India marketed its weaknesses as restraint and
would have been unable to take back the peaks had the withdrawal
not occurred. These views again are significant for two reasons, both
disturbing because of their variance with the facts. First, the Pakistani Army's defeat at Kargil is attributed to the venality of Pakistan's
politicians—a Pakistani version of the post-1918 German "stab-in-
the-back" theory—and not the strategic, operational, and tactical
blunders of the soldiers who planned, organized, and executed the
operation in the field. Second, the failure to appreciate the Indian
Army's operational and tactical successes in the costly eviction campaign is compounded by pervasive ignorance of the extensive Indian
preparations for horizontal escalation, preparations that were initiated both as a prudent measure in case of Pakistani attack and as a

---

[8]Shireen M. Mazari, "Kargil: Misguided Perceptions," Pakistan Institute for Air
Defence Studies, n.d. (available at www.piads.com.pk/users/piads/mazari1.html).

mitigatory strategy in case the eviction efforts along the occupied heights were not as successful as they eventually turned out to be.

If, on balance, these three beliefs represent merely a psychological rationalization aimed at snatching some semblance of victory from what was otherwise a national humiliation, they would have little significance from the perspective of stability. If these beliefs—despite being fundamentally false in their details—represent considered assessments held by Pakistan's national security establishment, however, the implications for stability are unsettling. They would reinforce the canard that Kargil was a military victory that Pakistan was done out of simply due to the actions of pusillanimous civilian leaders acting in concert with a hostile United States, and the perpetuation of such beliefs could, with the passage of time, give rise to policies that attempt Kargil-like operations in the future, which could lead to more disastrous consequences.

Pakistan Must More Effectively Assess and Gauge International Reaction

There is widespread consensus that Pakistan failed to predict strategically the international response to the conflict and the implications that this response would have for the execution of the Kargil operation. The Kargil crisis and its sequelae demonstrated Pakistan's endemic inability to anticipate international opinion and that opinion's operational implications, as is reflected by the views of high-level officers in the uniformed military and foreign office bureaucrats (who incidentally denied any active role of the Pakistani Army). Of course, the larger issue is the systemic deficiencies seemingly inherent in Pakistan's grand strategy that permit Pakistan to launch military operations that are not supported by strategic assessment of all possible outcomes and their probabilities. This view of deficient assessment generally, and with regard to Kargil in particular, was expressed by a wide range of public opinion shapers and analysts.[9]

---

[9] M. B. Naqvi, "Looking Beyond Kargil"; Gen-Maj. (Retd) M. Akbar, "Time for Sober Reflection"; Shahid M. Amin, "Kargil: The Unanswered Questions II—Time to Shed Illusions."

Pakistan's strategic objectives in prosecuting the Kargil operation were explicated by retired army officers, political leadership, and analysts. One strategic objective was the internationalization of the Kashmir issue. By reminding the international community that Kashmir is a potential nuclear flashpoint, Pakistan hoped to rouse the comity of nations—particularly the United States and China—to force a peace process in Kashmir. A second strategic goal was the interdiction of the National Highway-1 to disrupt India's supply lines to Siachen. (Some interlocutors suggested that this was to retaliate against India for its repeated shelling of the Neelum Valley road, a problem that has forced Pakistan to develop an alternate route to the region.) Some informants also conjectured that Pakistan assumed that India, with its weakened government, would not likely respond.[10] Pakistan radically misread the political resolve of Vajpayee and the political pressure put on him to respond in light of the forthcoming elections and the popular outrage in India precipitated by the occupation in the post-Lahore environment. Several interlocutors speculated that the government assumed that the international community would intervene within a few days or weeks (as had been the case in previous India-Pakistan conflicts) in the possible event that India perceived the operation as an act of war and reacted conventionally. A third goal was to give a fillip to the diminished morale among the mujahideen in the valley and to demonstrate that Pakistan's recently confirmed nuclear capabilities did have strategic benefits in that they allowed Islamabad to undertake more-active military operations in support of the Kashmiri cause without inordinate fear of Indian reprisals.

To the extent that these objectives hinged on specific expectations of the international environment, the question that must be asked is why Pakistan thought that its operations would be greeted with support or at least understanding. Writers in Pakistani English newspapers were also apparently unable to understand the government's misguided strategic calculus. An article written by Aziz Siddiqui in *The Dawn* captured this sentiment. Siddiqui speculated that planners may have believed no one could be held responsible for "independent mujahideen actions." However, he also said that "this may be true for something on a guerilla scale. But it is a different

---

[10]See also Altaf Gauhar, "Four Wars, One Assumption."

matter to hold a stationary position that threatens enemy supply lines."[11] While this analysis cannot fully explicate why Pakistan was so confident, one possible reason is that Pakistan may have been emboldened by the sympathy that the United States expressed for Islamabad after India's nuclear tests and Pakistan's subsequently constrained response.

Given Pakistan's dubious assertions that Kargil was simply a mujahideen operation, the natural question arises as to whether Pakistan expected that the United States would not detect the presence of Pakistani regular forces in Kargil. And if Pakistan did at all expect the United States to uncover the truth of the operation, did Pakistan expect that the United States would not make this information known? Again, based on the expectation that U.S. support expressed in the aftermath of the Indian nuclear tests was durable and enduring, Pakistan may have launched the Kargil operation in part thinking that this action would be perceived abroad—even if its true contours were understood—as an expression of Pakistan's disenchantment with the desultory Indian approach on Kashmir and as "just deserts" for all the burdens New Delhi imposed on Islamabad as a result of its nuclear tests. One important consequence of this fact for U.S.-Pakistan relations may be the continual prospect of "the tail wagging the dog," that is, any overt demonstration of U.S. support for some Pakistani geopolitical goals runs the risk of Islamabad's carrying out destabilizing actions intended to exploit that support.

Clearly, one reading of events suggests that at each node of the decision tree, Pakistan made unrealistic assessments about the range of possible outcomes. Fundamentally, Pakistan did not anticipate the intolerance that the international community—especially the United States and China—would demonstrate for its attempts to alter the status quo even if the community was otherwise sympathetic to its dilemmas in the face of India's nuclear tests.

A retired general offered a different—but important—interpretation of what has often been understood as Pakistan's seemingly astrategic prosecution of Kargil. He argued that Pakistan understood very well

---

[11]Aziz Siddiqui, "Downhill from Kargil," *The Dawn*, June 29, 1999.

the risks but felt compelled to take a calculated gamble in an attempt to alter the status quo—*precisely because it perceived that it had no other choices.*[12] By this logic, if Pakistan always acted according to the anticipated end game, it would never do anything to secure its interests, because all the strategic options available to Islamabad are invariably unattractive.[13] This view has serious strategic consequences: it implies that Pakistan may be in many ways like prewar Japan—a country that has few good choices but is nonetheless constrained to act in what may appear to be an inexplicable way because it finds itself in a position where the bad option is, from its perspective, the best of the poor alternatives available. The implications of this logic for Pakistani decisionmaking in the nuclear age are entirely unsettling.

Need for Broad Assessment and Review of Proposed Operations

Several interlocutors explained that at the most basic level, Kargil was a military operation and its planners largely failed to predict both India's military response to the Pakistani occupation and the diplomatic consequences. For the planners of Kargil, this appeared to be a low-risk, low-cost operation. However, the Pakistani military establishment (and, for that matter, the Pakistani state) does not have the capability to fully assess the full range of costs and benefits. Thus, several editorialists have called for a body akin to an NSC that would comprise the leading organs of the state as well as opposition leadership.

M. P. Bhandara, a columnist for *The Dawn*, wrote one of the more thorough discussions of an NSC and its presumed role in assessing an operation like Kargil.[14] In Bhandara's formulation, the Foreign

---

[12]It could be argued, of course, that Pakistan did have other choices, but none that it considered palatable or was willing to accept.

[13]The range, and limitations, of the strategic choices available to Pakistan has been examined in some detail in Ashley J. Tellis, "The Changing Political-Military Environment: South Asia," in Zalmay Khalilzad et al., *The United States and Asia: Toward a New U.S. Strategy and Force Posture* (Santa Monica, California: RAND, 2001), pp. 218–224.

[14]M. P. Bhandara, "On the Edge of the Precipice," *The Dawn*, July 21, 1999.

Office would argue that Kargil would enable India to "expose Pakistan as an aggressor and a fundamentalist state," allowing India to regain much of the diplomatic clout it forfeited with its nuclear tests. Indeed, Kargil would be a boon to India, as New Delhi would easily make use of the crisis to position itself as a front-line state against Islamist terrorism. The Finance Ministry would argue that Kargil would precipitate a cutoff by the World Bank, the International Monetary Fund (IMF), and the G-8. The Joint Chiefs of Staff would have the opportunity to assess realistically a local battle in Kashmir, considering the possibility of an unpredictable expansion. The main function of such a body would be to assess the costs and benefits of such adventurism in terms of its economic, political, military, international, and regional consequences. The author lucidly concludes: "The downside price paid by Pakistan at Kargil would have been rated [by the NSC] as simply too high in the context of any possible upside scenario."[15]

At the heart of these calls for such a body is the understanding that Pakistan needs to expand its understanding of costs to include the opportunity costs of social, political, and economic development that are derailed by Pakistan's policy of supporting jihadi elements in the Kashmir insurgency. These policies impose many other costs as well, especially with respect to Pakistan's ability to foster an image as a responsible nuclear state. India, despite suffering much as a result of Pakistan's Kashmir policy, was a solid beneficiary of Pakistan's Kargil operation insofar as that conflict allowed the international community to compare India's cautiousness and restraint with Pakistan's recklessness and provocation—comparisons that in Pakistan's case are unfortunately increasingly intertwined with images of state failure, Islamist terrorism, internal corruption, and political decay. Some key Pakistani journalists and political leaders have extended the notion of opportunity costs even further: they have asserted that Kargil has in fact laid the groundwork for legitimizing highly proactive Indian solutions to the Kashmir problem, such as crossing the LOC and striking deep into Pakistani Kashmir.

The absence of an NSC-like organ in Pakistan cannot account for the inability of Nawaz Sharif—a seasoned politician—to think through

---

[15]Ibid.

these issues and conclude that the misadventurous Kargil plan would have deleterious consequences. The facile conclusion often drawn is that Nawaz Sharif was not capable of understanding complicated end games, but a more challenging explanation would focus on the deeply conflicted relationship between the civilian government and the military, the imprecise boundaries of mutual autonomy in matters of grand strategy, and the role of specific personalities in any given political-military crisis.[16] (This suggests that Kargil might not have been executed or might have been executed very differently if there had been a different mix of personalities at the helm in Pakistan.) Thus, it is important to recognize that without effective civilian leadership structures, a stable balance of power within the Pakistani state, and a clear political will and intentions, even an NSC-like body could not preclude a Kargil-like scenario from occurring. Reflecting upon the explanation proffered by the retired general referred to earlier, it is not obvious that such a body would recommend against the prosecution of such an operation when launched as a strategic risk—if it were to be dominated by unaccountable bureaucracies that are convinced Pakistan must act even when Islamabad is confronted by nothing but poor alternatives.

Pakistan Needs a Media Strategy to Shape Opinion

Many informants and opinion shapers contrasted the facility with which India gained the upper hand on the information battlefield to Pakistan's deficiencies in this arena. These individuals pointed out the need to develop media policies that would give Pakistan a greater ability to convincingly communicate its position and official version of events to its own populace and to the international community.[17]

As suggested above, all of Pakistan's putative strategic objectives were highly contingent on specific expectations of how key players

---

[16]It should be noted that as far as Sharif was concerned, almost his entire second "term" as Prime Minister was focused on preventing a dismissal from office, which occurred during his first term and, as is now acknowledged, on accumulating personal gain. In such circumstances, it is unlikely that he sought outside counsel on matters of state or asked the necessary hard questions of the military himself.

[17]See, for example, Mahdi Masud, "Kargil Crisis: A Balance Sheet" (also carried by the Pakistan Institute for Air Defence Studies). See also Arif Shamin, "War on the Net," *The News,* July 11, 1999.

such as India, the United States, and China would react. Surely, Pakistan's inability to anticipate the international reaction was deeply problematic. However, Pakistan's failure to influence the international reaction was also seen to be problematic by its political elites—a view reiterated on numerous occasions in our interviews. While this conviction is understandable, it is important to recognize that not many interlocutors appreciated the fact that even the most effective media strategy in the context of the Kargil war could not hope to influence the international community in the long run if the bedrock of Pakistan's claims consisted essentially of lies that were not sufficiently recognized within Pakistan.

Some political figures reasoned that Pakistan's inability to shape international opinion proactively was due to the deep secrecy with which Kargil was conducted, and concluded that Pakistan cannot conduct operations like Kargil without a broad-based consensus across the various governmental and military institutions. Several retired army officers and political leaders opined that the canard of the army's noninvolvement contributed to the deep distrust of Pakistan in international forums. In this context, it was argued that the international community would have understood Pakistan's objectives better had Islamabad been forthright about the operation and made the case that India has on numerous occasions violated the LOC in Siachen, Chorbat La, Qamar, and elsewhere. Thus, Pakistan could have cast the Kargil operation as an extension of Siachen, which may have garnered more support internationally.

It is important to understand the extent to which Kargil was perceived to be an extension of Siachen, which Pakistan argues is an illegal occupation in contravention of the Shimla Agreement. A wide range of interlocutors made the point that no one should have been surprised by Kargil insofar as it followed "naturally" from Siachen. Many Pakistanis seemed to believe that the international community would make this link intuitively and support Pakistan—or, at a minimum, take no notice of the operation. In asserting this claim, however, these interlocutors appear to have put much stock in the belief that the international community either cares greatly about minor military operations at obscure locations such as Chorbat La and Qamar or is convinced about the validity of Pakistan's grievances with respect to Siachen.[18]

In any event, while many critics argued the need to counter India's media machine, a number of concerns arose about the ways in which information on this operation was disseminated domestically. Reflecting the international and domestic distrust of the government, one editorialist wrote incredulously on the misinformation campaign against domestic and international audiences:

> We are told incessantly that the Kargil freedom fighters are genuine Kashmiri freedom fighters. However, is it reasonable to believe that freedom fighters can fight at 15,000 feet above sea level without Pakistani rations, clothing, logistics, ammunition and intelligence support? Again, who are we fooling? It is possible for PTV to beguile

---

[18]Pakistan did try to make this case. However, it did so late in the crisis in what appeared to be an insubstantial ex post facto rationalization of the operation in international forums. Pakistan's ability to make this case convincingly had numerous shortcomings. First, there is a paucity of public information about the alleged Qamar and Chorbat La incidents, and Pakistan could only provide scant data about these incidents. Second, there is little documentation of Pakistan's protesting these incidents at the time of their occurrence. Third, the terrain in question (and the Indian penetrations, if they occurred) in the Qamar and Chorbat La incidents was not sufficiently substantial to provoke a robust international response, which may make these incidents incomparable to the larger-scale Kargil incident. Fourth, assuming Pakistani claims are true, these incidents occurred in a very different international context from that of Kargil; they occurred prior to the formal nuclearization of the subcontinent and well before the attempted rapprochement represented by Lahore took place. Finally, these events (which arguably occurred in 1972 and 1988, respectively) lacked currency and thus appeared to be a pallid motivation for prosecuting the Kargil operation in 1999. The Indian operations in Siachen, however, represent an exception to this conclusion as there is considerable information about India's occupation of Siachen. The legal status of this occupation, however, is ambiguous because of the imprecise language in the India-Pakistani agreement demarcating the territory north of Point NJ 9842. (For more on this issue, see Jasjit Singh, "Battle for Siachen: Beginning of the Third War," in Jasjit Singh (ed.), *Kargil 1999: Pakistan's Fourth War for Kashmir* (New Delhi: Knowledge World, 1999), pp. 60–88; Lt. Gen. (Retd) Dr. M. L. Chibber, "Siachen—The Untold Story," *Indian Defence Review*, January 1990; Robert G. Wirsing, "The Siachen Dispute: Can Diplomacy Untangle It?" *Indian Defence Review*, July 1991.) While invoking these incidents to justify the prosecution of Kargil may seem like an "excuse" grounded in a post factum defensiveness, evidence gathered from interviews and from the literature review strongly supports the notion that these incidents are critical to Pakistan's public mythology about Kashmir, India's behavior in Kashmir, and Islamabad's justification for Kargil.

its captive audience at home but the world does not consists [sic] of retards [sic].[19]

This same author situates Kargil within the landscape of Pakistani adventurism and misrepresentations dating back to the 1947 war with India. One interlocutor, a retired general, aired irritation with the government's story and succinctly argued that Pakistanis had a right to know that their troops were fighting and dying in Kargil. Even Shireen Mazari wrote critically about the inability of the state to "take its people into confidence on crucial policy matters."[20]

Although several informants expressed considerable interest in Pakistan's becoming better situated to influence international opinion, it remains unclear whether there are efforts under way to build this capacity. Moreover, there are serious limitations imposed upon the efficacy of such a strategy, even if the capacity to carry it out existed in the first place. The most important limitation on such efforts derives, first and foremost, from the very legitimacy of the use of violence to achieve Pakistan's political objectives and from Pakistan's continuing perception that violence—whether unleashed through conventional operations, low-intensity wars waged by proxy, or state-sponsored terrorism—is necessary to achieve its political objectives vis-à-vis India. Pakistan will no doubt persist in its support of insurgency in Kashmir, since this is seen as one of the few low-cost options Islamabad has versus New Delhi, and it is far from clear what impact an enhanced media strategy could have when such a policy increasingly finds disfavor in international politics. Further, even the best media strategy would be inutile in the long run in sustaining a fallacious cover story.

Pakistan's Options Are Limited to the Pursuit of Low Intensity Conflict

A wide range of interlocutors, including uniformed and retired army officers, present and former diplomats, analysts, and journalists, explained that in their view Pakistan's options to bring about a favor-

---

[19]M.P. Bhandara, "On the Edge of the Precipice."
[20]Shireen M. Mazari, "Re-Examining Kargil."

able resolution in Kashmir are highly limited. Kargil-like operations cannot be prosecuted at will, because they are inherently risky and costly. Diplomatically, Pakistan recognizes that the initiative will remain with India in part because Pakistan cannot marshal international influence to bear upon India.

Yet Pakistan desperately wants to change the status quo. Pakistan deeply fears that India will be able to coerce it into converting the LOC as the international border, and these fears become more salient as India continues along its currently ascendant path. Thus, there is wide concurrence in Pakistan that violence remains Pakistan's only option if the current peace opening is not productive. Nearly all informants indicated that Pakistan's only viable option for bringing India to the negotiating table is to continue to calibrate the heat of the insurgency within Kashmir. It is presumed that this LIC strategy will over time tire the Indian Army by affecting its PERSTEMPO (Personnel Tempo), OPSTEMPO (Operations Tempo), and morale. It is expected that once India's will to fight has been vitiated, India will become amenable to resolving the Kashmir issue on terms more favorable to Pakistan. However, few Pakistanis appear to recognize the inherent long-term challenges of this strategy, and many have succumbed to the illusion that India is tiring with respect to Kashmir.

While it is important to understand the extent to which Pakistan is dissatisfied with the status quo, it also should be pointed out that a few interlocutors did in fact suggest that Pakistan's minimal requirements for resolving the Kashmir issue could be as little as "the LOC plus or minus." One academic analyst even went so far as to suggest that Musharraf ultimately believed that this was the only realistic option. Another political leader emphasized that both Pakistan and India need an honorable way out of this impasse: *"Any change in the status quo can be claimed as a victory."* While these views are consoling, it is far from obvious that they are held by a broad swath of individual stakeholders.

Most Pakistanis recognize that the struggle of Kashmir today, including the use of jihadi forces in the fight, is complicated by other considerations, such as the desire to be responsive to the disenchantment of the Kashmiris, the opportunity to provide gainful employment to some of the Islamist mercenaries currently operating within Pakistan, and the perceived necessity to keep India pre-occupied with Kashmir lest it shift its superior military resources to threatening Pakistan directly. Despite all these considerations, however, many Pakistanis have become increasingly aware of the painful costs of the Kashmir war for Pakistan's own domestic stability, economic growth, and international image. The alternatives to Islamabad's current strategy, however, are not easy, given the historical legacies of the India-Pakistan conflict, the dominance of the Pakistan military in national decisionmaking, and the internal challenges facing the Pakistani state.

Nonetheless, the Kargil episode has fomented a nascent debate among the security elite with respect to Pakistan's well-known policy position calling for a plebiscite in Kashmir and the implementation of other UN resolutions. In a recent article,[21] Alexander Evans, a Western analyst, has in fact argued that the voices of what he calls "modernists"[22] have inveighed more loudly now that Pakistan's position is no longer relevant internationally. These modernists argue that Pakistan should focus on promoting self-determination of the Kashmiris, which implies that Pakistan should entertain independence for Kashmir as an option. (Abdul Sattar's statements in December 2000 that Pakistan would entertain the third option of independence may reflect this growing modernist influence.) They contend that the "best current option for Pakistan . . . is letting the best argument have its day in the court of Kashmiri public opinion."[23] Some modernists have even proposed reducing support for the jihadis, arguing that Kashmir's disposition will not be solved through military action alone. Still others have become unsympathetic to the national obsession with Kashmir itself because they contend that Pakistan's fate hinges upon investors, reformers, and

---

[21]Alexander Evans, "Reducing Tension Is Not Enough," *The Washington Quarterly*, Vol. 24, No. 2, 2001, pp. 181–193.

[22]Evans's use of the terms *modernists* and *traditionalists* in this recent article is unusual in the context of Pakistan. Rather than indexing a commitment to Islamicization (or some other religious frame of reference), these terms identify positions with respect to Pakistan's Kashmir policy. Modernists are those who are receptive to new formulations in Pakistan's Kashmir policy (e.g., recognizing the third option of Kashmiri independence); traditionalists are those who resist moving away from Pakistan's historical stance out of fear that any relaxation of this position will result in a de-internationalization of the problem.

[23]Alexander Evans, "Reducing Tension Is Not Enough," p. 186.

multilateral lending agencies—as much as it does on the ruling generals.[24]

Conversely, Evans's "traditionalists" steadfastly cling to Pakistan's 54-year-old policy position, arguing that any concession will precipitate a de-internationalization of Kashmir that will eventually permit India to "absorb" Kashmir. The traditionalists also reject the modernists' suggestions for diminishing (covert) support for the militancy, as such reduction would give India an upper hand.[25] To date, these views appear to remain dominant with respect to Pakistan's policy on Kashmir.

Nuclear Capabilities Become Key to the Successful Execution of Pakistan's Political Strategies

The Kargil crisis highlighted the critical importance of nuclear weapons to the success of Pakistan's grand strategy at multiple levels. To begin with, Pakistan's possession of nuclear weapons functioned as the critical *permissive* condition that made contemplating Kargil possible. The Indian decision to resume nuclear testing in May 1998 provided Pakistan—for all its encumbrances—with an incredible opportunity: first, to technically validate the weaponry it had assiduously sought to create since 1972; and second, to conclusively demonstrate to the world at large and particularly to India that Pakistan possesses capabilities previously only suspected (and in India often denigrated). The new public recognition of Pakistan's nuclear capabilities—as evidenced through Pakistan's tests in May 1998—provided Pakistan's leadership with new windows of opportunity and more-robust forms of immunity. Under the shadow of this public recognition, Pakistan could continue to pursue its objective of "strategic diversion," that is, enervating India through the mechanism of LIC even as it pursued more positive goals such as attempting to secure Kashmir.

In addition to the permissive role they play, nuclear weapons are also critical for another reason: they function as the means by which

---

[24]Ibid., pp. 186–187.
[25]Ibid.

Pakistan can ward off the worst Indian counter-responses that could be precipitated by Islamabad's attempts at strategic diversion. Nuclear weapons play this role in two ways: first, they are straightforward deterrents to any Indian conventional and nuclear threats that may materialize in a crisis, and second, they are perfect instruments for catalyzing international intervention on Pakistan's behalf should a South Asian political-military crisis threaten to spin out of control. Given the "defensive" and "catalytic" utility of nuclear weapons, three conclusions about these weapons appear to have been drawn by Pakistani policymakers. First, Pakistan may require the largest, most diversified, and most effective nuclear arsenal possible, because the exploitation of nuclear weaponry to secure certain political goals requires more than just token nuclear capabilities. Second, Pakistan may need to prepare and mobilize its nuclear reserves—at least selectively to begin with—early in a crisis for purely defensive reasons in the face of potential Indian counteraction or conventional preemption. This may include crisis alerting, physical dispersal of assets, and possibly preparing weapons and delivery systems for nuclear operations. Third, all the actions connected with this process have the very beneficial result of tacitly signaling to India the seriousness of Pakistan's deterrent threat even as they help to catalyze international intervention to resolve the crisis—to Pakistan's advantage, it is hoped.

These three dimensions of Pakistan's nuclear calculus were evident during the Kargil crisis. A highly placed Pakistani civil servant privately accepted—even if he found it difficult to openly admit—that the Kargil operation was rooted in many important ways in the protection that Pakistan's newly acknowledged nuclear capabilities provided. Further, he also noted that many senior Pakistani military officers associated with the planning for this operation believe that these same capabilities prevented a wider and more intense war even as they served to catalyze U.S. diplomatic interest in bringing the conflict to a conclusion—though perhaps not in the way desired by Islamabad.

INDIA'S PERSPECTIVE

India Must Prepare for Future Pakistani Recklessness Across-the-Board

A wide array of Indian policymakers, analysts, and opinion makers expressed the need to be ready for Pakistani adventurism that could successively manifest itself in several issue areas. One senior Indian strategist captured this sentiment by using Mohammed of Ghori as a leitmotif: Ghori apparently made sixteen unsuccessful attempts at capturing the Rajput centers of power in North India before succeeding on the seventeenth try by unfair means. The moral of the story, according to this analyst, is that Pakistan's defeat at Kargil (and possibly future defeats as well) would only whet its appetite for further attempts at coercion, and if success did not accrue to traditional means of attack, nontraditional stratagems were to be expected. One such stratagem, which was of great concern to policymakers, was the spread of terrorism throughout India. (Indeed, interviews in Pakistan confirmed reason for such concern.) The December 2000 attack on the Red Fort could become a foretaste of things to come as jihadi groups expand their areas of operation beyond the state of Jammu and Kashmir. Pakistan was also anticipated to increase its low-intensity activities in the valley itself and in Kashmir more generally. And as shown, this too is consistent with Pakistan's expressed intentions.

Another stratagem of concern involved possible Pakistani activity using air or naval assets in novel and hitherto unseen forms for conventional operations and shallow incursions intended to probe Indian defenses and possibly force New Delhi to overreact. Other individuals, especially in the Indian intelligence community, argued that India has to brace itself for other nontraditional threats. Some of these "asymmetric strategies" were seen to include the increasing Inter-Service Intelligence (ISI) activities in Nepal and in India's northeastern states, which are rife with insurgency. Another operational possibility mentioned was economic subversion, perhaps through counterfeiting and other black-market operations. Finally, it was feared that Pakistan, again through its ISI, might try to exploit dissatisfaction in India's numerous subaltern populations, such as the Muslim underclass, the Dalits, and other marginalized social groups. Irrespective of the kind of threat at issue, almost all Indian policymakers were of the opinion that Pakistan's defeat at Kargil did not imply the abdication of its traditional objective of weakening India. Rather, the defeat at Kargil was only likely to catalyze the Pakistani imagination in more fervid ways and precipitate a search for more novel means of attacking Indian interests.

India Must Increase Its Efforts to Contain Intrusions Across the LOC

The *Kargil Review Committee Report* highlights the doubts many military planners had regarding India's ability to respond effectively against a large Pakistani intrusion. The fear was based on the disposition of Indian forces throughout the country and the perceived inability to respond logistically to an unexpected Pakistani foray. The decisive Indian response to the Pakistani cross-border threat demonstrated to India that it has the inherent capability to counter a well-organized military threat from Pakistan even when Pakistan has the advantage of surprise.[26] Not everyone, however, saw the victory as unequivocal. Rather, "the structure and conditions of the withdrawal [rendered] what most likely would have been an unconditional military victory into a profoundly complex and problematic one."[27]

Although India claimed military and political success after Kargil, the conflict precipitated serious concerns about current capabilities. The intelligence failure and the idea that harsh weather kept the military from identifying the incursion more swiftly highlighted the need to invest in more-robust military, logistics, and intelligence equipment and personnel in order to deter and counter future attacks.

As fully detailed in the *Kargil Review Committee Report,* and as echoed by those interviewed in the political-military establishment and the intelligence agencies themselves, the Indian government will begin to investigate the current approach along the LOC and invest heavily in the type of materiel necessary to create a robust forward defense with the ability to inflict great costs on the Pakistani army if required. Several Indian military officers described the need for ad-

---

[26]Arpit Rajain, "India's Political and Diplomatic Response to the Kargil Crisis," p. 11.

[27]Parveen Swami, *The Kargil War* (New Delhi: LeftWord Books, 1999), p. 19.

vanced sensors, better communications technologies, and more-effective quick-reaction capabilities if India is to avoid having to create the equivalent of a "great wall" along the LOC. As a way to secure operational advantage, many Indian military officers argued, such solutions promise better dividends in comparison to alternative strategies such as permanently forward-deploying forces along the perimeter, especially the more inhospitable portions of the LOC. As part of this search for alternatives, senior Indian civilian and military officers described the need for upgrading the transportation infrastructure in Kashmir. This includes the need for more all-weather roads, better alternative routes to the currently vulnerable internal lines of communication, more-secure stockpiling of arms and ammunition, and better intratheater airlift.

The Kashmir Issue Requires High-Level Attention

High-level Indian stakeholders indicated that the Kashmir issue requires high-level attention and commitment in addition to creative responses on the part of the Indian state for resolving the ongoing insurgency. India understands clearly that the Kashmir issue will not diminish or atrophy if left unattended.

In this vein, India is attempting to pursue a dialog with all Kashmiris, especially select constituencies such as the more moderate members of the All Parties Hurriyat Conference (APHC). This high-level strategic effort is being orchestrated by the Prime Minister's Office—signaling the importance of the issue. This is in contrast to the more tactical concerns of the Jammu and Kashmir Affairs Department, which has resided in the Home Ministry's Office since May 1998.[28] India thus seems to be pursuing high-level strategic engagements with key Kashmiri elements as a way to reach resolution while still attempting to deal firmly with the insurgency at the tactical level.

Because the Kashmir crisis involves law-and-order issues, military operations, economic renewal, the political revitalization of state politics, and interstate relations (including those with Pakistan), the Indian national leadership is convinced that high-level attention

---

[28]"J&K's Return to Home Signals Change in Policy," *The Hindustan Times Online Edition*, May 26, 1998.

alone can produce progress that resolves the issue. Many early ideas, such as leaving the state government to take the lead in restoring normalcy, have by now been completely abandoned, and responsibility for managing the Kashmir issue in its many dimensions now lies directly in the Prime Minister's Office with key national leaders such as the foreign, defence, and home ministers and the national security advisor. If the current dialog with Pakistan gathers steam, this process of centralized high-level attention to Kashmir will only be further reinforced.

India Must Cultivate International Support That Will Circumscribe Pakistani Adventurism

India understands well that the extent of international support it received during the crisis was contingent upon circumstances and will be so in the future.[29] India also knows that it cannot take the durability of such a supportive environment for granted and consequently must work consistently to create an international environment that is conducive to its strategic interests. Thus, India will likely pursue a dual-pronged strategy. India will undertake multifaceted efforts that foster a positive international opinion of India as a responsible nuclear state, capable of restraint and interested in peace. However, India will also seek to retain its operational independence insofar as dealing with the insurgency is concerned, since it cannot rely solely on the existence of a positive international environment to limit the damage that might be done to it by both domestic and foreign insurgents as well as by Pakistan. The potential tension that might be inherent in these two strategies implies that the former will serve to put real brakes on India's propensity, low though it might be to begin with, to deal with its adversaries in overly violent ways. This implies that for external reasons alone, there are strong incentives for India not to pursue more "proactive" solutions to the Kashmiri insurgency, including cross-border attacks, limited aims wars, and offensive air operations. The pressure to avoid international opprobrium also implies that any aggressive Indian responses to Pakistani provocations are likely to be both covert and scaled in intensity to the challenge they are meant to neuter. This

---

[29]Arpit Rajain, "India's Political and Diplomatic Response to the Kargil Crisis," p. 14.

issue is explored further in Chapter Four, in the section addressing India's future options.

India Must Sustain the Information Offensive

The media were continually cited as a relevant factor in influencing public opinion domestically and internationally. (Respondents in Pakistan made much of India's media strategy and its importance in seizing the diplomatic victory.) The *Kargil Review Committee Report* urges the Indian military to take a stronger role in educating and assisting the media in areas where military operations are unfolding. The lack of a well-articulated perception management campaign and the lack of a comprehensive set of guidelines for handling the media were listed as key deficiencies in the civil-military apparatus that need to be addressed by India. The *Kargil Review Committee Report* lays out a more specific civil-military approach to be implemented for future operations.[30]

India has a good understanding of the multiple uses of a well-planned media management strategy. For example, Major General Arjun Ray describes the complex role of the media in prosecuting a national strategy with respect to insurgency and terrorism in the *Kashmir Diary*. Ray writes: "[T]he political and operational objectives of the national strategy for fighting militancy and terrorism have to be disseminated to target audiences, coordinated at all levels and monitored continuously."[31] In addition, it may be understood when reading the *Kargil Review Committee Report* that the Committee clearly sees the value in the media's ability to shape both domestic and international perceptions. As a result, the use of information warfare techniques and the intentional use of the private media to mold perceptions in future operations will be thoughtfully considered by members of the Indian political, military, and intelligence groups at all echelons.

---

[30]India Kargil Review Committee, *From Surprise to Reckoning: The Kargil Review Committee Report*, pp. 214–219.

[31]Maj. Gen. Arjun Ray, *Kashmir Diary: Psychology of Militancy.* Also see Pegasus, "Insurgency and Counter-Insurgency: The Anatomy of an Insurgent Movement and Counter Measures"; Lt. Gen. Vijay Madan, "Population Terrain—The Neglected Factor of Counter-Insurgency Operations."

India's experience in Kargil demonstrated that effective media and opinion-shaping policies could affect both Indian and Pakistani operations. The international reaction to the Kargil crisis bolstered India's position with respect to Kargil specifically and perhaps toward Kashmir generally. The U.S., Chinese, and G-8 responses to the Kargil events were perceived to signal the international community's support for Indian restraint while condemning Pakistani aggression. India concluded that it must consistently convey its policy of responsibility and restraint while simultaneously describing its condition of victimization to international audiences. The *Kargil Review Committee Report* clearly reflects this notion:

> Pakistan for its part has become the fount of religious extremism and international terrorism and a patron of the global narcotics traffic. Decades of misgovernance and military rule have prevented the democratic tradition from taking firm root. In consequence, Pakistan poses a threat not only to India but to its other neighbors as well. . . .[T]errorists have carried out murderous assaults in the United States and East Africa.[32]

This passage summarizes the Indian view of Pakistan as the source of instability in South Asia and beyond. This is a critical element of India's strategic perceptions, and Pakistan's own political choices during the last decade amply corroborate such depictions.

Domestic support of operations in Kargil was also demonstrable, as reflected by the generous contributions made to the Army Welfare Fund. Support, in various forms, came from across a variety of constituencies. As Rajain writes, "There were no communal flare-ups. Even the various insurgent groups all over the country chose not to take the sheen away from an emphatic Indian victory."[33] This wellspring of support demonstrated to the Indian military and government that providing the public with information can be an important tool to help cultivate domestic support, and the numerous studies of

---

[32]India Kargil Review Committee, *From Surprise to Reckoning: The Kargil Review Committee Report*, p. 222.

[33]Arpit Rajain, "India's Political and Diplomatic Response to the Kargil Crisis," p. 21.

the Kargil crisis now being published in India[34] will enable New Delhi to do even better with respect to perception management than it did the last time around.

India Must Treat Nuclear Issues More Seriously

Although Indian policymakers do not wish to advertise the fact that Pakistan issued "tacit" nuclear threats during the Kargil crisis— mainly because doing so only serves to reinforce the value of Pakistan's nuclear coercion—many key figures in the Prime Minister's Office, the ministries of External Affairs and Defence, and the Indian military admitted that it was so. These threats were viewed as articulated through both the (formally) ambiguous but nonetheless unsettling statements issued by senior Pakistani policymakers and the "activation" of at least one Pakistani missile base and the possible readying of several missile systems.[35] Despite the fact that the Kargil operation was a geographically limited affair, Pakistan's tacit issuance of nuclear threats was read in New Delhi as perfectly consistent with Islamabad's larger grand strategy: exploiting its nuclear capabilities to underwrite limited conflicts even as it seeks to limit Indian counteraction and catalyze international intervention.[36]

Precisely because even a limited conflict such as Kargil manifested Pakistan's willingness to actively exploit its nuclear assets, Indian policymakers drew several conclusions of significant consequence. First, they believe that India must take nuclear issues seriously along multiple dimensions: develop the capabilities necessary to sustain

---

[34]Such monographs include Col. Ravi Nanda, *Kargil: A Wakeup Call*; Air Commodore Jasjit Singh, *Kargil 1999—Pakistan's Fourth War for Kashmir*; and Col. (Retd) Bhaskar Sarkar, *Kargil War: Past, Present and Future.*

[35]Raj Chengappa, "Pakistan Threatened India with Nuclear Attack: Army Chief," *The Newspaper Today*, January 12, 2001.

[36]A chronological reconstruction of Pakistan's nuclear threats, however, suggests that these signals were issued primarily *after* India began its conventional military mobilization and redeployment in response to the Kargil incursion. This mobilization and redeployment was certainly initiated for precautionary reasons, but once completed, it would have enabled India to mount a variety of punitive operations—operations that Islamabad might have been sufficiently concerned about to issue nuclear threats. Because this explanation overlaps with the alternative Indian argument about Pakistan's interest in catalytic intervention, it is difficult to choose between the two on the basis of unclassified data alone.

the "minimum credible deterrent," complete the institutional reorganization necessary to manage India's emerging nuclear capabilities, and plan seriously for the prospect of either deliberate or inadvertent nuclear breakdown. Second, they believe that the Indian national security establishment needs a better appreciation of Pakistan's nuclear capabilities, the production infrastructure contributing to these capabilities, the key personalities—especially at mid-level—involved in these efforts, and the nature, durability, and extent of Pakistan's links with its principal external suppliers. Third, they believe that Pakistan's willingness to exploit its nuclear weaponry for even the most mundane ends might require India to consider developing at least a small set of rapid-response capabilities primarily for shoring up deterrence and "concentrating the mind" of Pakistani decisionmakers who might be tempted to behave irresponsibly in a crisis. Several Indian reports insinuated that New Delhi had readied such nuclear capabilities during the crisis as a precautionary measure.[37] All told, the Kargil conflict appears to have altered the images Indian policymakers traditionally held about the role, necessity, and significance of nuclear weapons in limited conflicts in South Asia. If these alterations lead to dramatic transformations in India's evolving nuclear posture, the Kargil crisis will have bequeathed a far more lasting legacy than might have otherwise been the case.

CONCLUSIONS

The most important lesson that Pakistan learned from Kargil is that Kargil-like operations have high political costs, especially in terms of Pakistan's international reputation. That said, however, the Kargil fiasco does not appear to have extinguished Pakistan's belief that violence, especially as expressed through support for the Kashmir insurgency, remains the best—if not the only effective—policy choice for pressuring India on Kashmir and other outstanding disputes. Perhaps because of such a belief, several constituencies in Pakistan continue to hold that the Kargil war, for all its high political costs, may have been a success lost. The tensions between these two positions—that Kargil, on one hand, was a political debacle and, on the

---

[37]For details, see Raj Chengappa, *Weapons of Peace: The Secret Story of India's Quest to Be a Nuclear Power* (New Delhi, India: Harper Collins, 2000).

other hand, represents a "lost victory" of some sort—were usually not explored at any length by interlocutors who have argued both points of view in private. At the very least, then, what is suggested is a profound ambiguity about Pakistan's final evaluation of the worth of the Kargil war, which makes it difficult to conclude *unambiguously* that the Kargil conflict is universally viewed in Pakistan as a cataclysmic event never to be repeated. Consequently, even though the dominant view in Pakistan currently appears to concede the failure of Kargil (and as such, it is hoped, will function as a deterrent to future operations of this nature), it is difficult to affirm conclusively that Kargil-like operations will never occur in South Asia. So long as Pakistan finds value in different kinds of subconventional violence for strategic purposes, the Kashmir dispute between India and Pakistan remains unresolved, and various pathologies of decisionmaking continue to manifest themselves within the region, it is possible—though not probable—that an unfavorable concatenation of circumstances could spur a Kargil-like event in the future.

What the Kargil fiasco certainly taught Pakistan was that its appreciation of the international environment was inadequate. A number of writers and informants suggested that an NSC-like body might preclude ill-advised operations or even restrain highly insular decisionmaking. A number of writers and interlocutors argued that Pakistan requires a media strategy, and some informants noted in private that the mujahideen cover story fed to the press was not productive for a variety of reasons. Nearly all interlocutors indicated, however, that because Pakistan feels that its diplomatic, political, and military options are highly restricted, its best option is to continue attempting to coerce India to the negotiating table through the low-intensity war in Kashmir. It is in this context that Pakistan's nuclear capabilities are seen to remain critical and, for all the reasons adumbrated earlier, are only likely to grow in significance for Pakistan.

The most important conclusion that India drew from Kargil is that India must be prepared to counter a wide range of Pakistani threats that may be mounted by what is essentially a reckless but tenacious adversary. In this context, India must develop the robust forward defense capabilities necessary to thwart surprise and to win even if surprised by Pakistan. Despite this need to prepare for future Pakistani adventurism, India has emerged from Kargil much more confident in that it believes it can handle Pakistan's worst aggression successfully even when it is relatively unprepared. India also appreciates that eliminating the prospect of future Kargil-like operations requires it to focus resolutely on resolving the Kashmir crisis, which in turn implies that the problem must be engaged at the highest level. India further recognizes the need to assiduously cultivate international support and that such support will only accrue to the degree that India both behaves responsibly and is seen to be behaving responsibly toward all its immediate neighbors. The Kargil war demonstrated abundantly that if India behaves as a responsible nuclear state, capable of restraint and desirous of peace, rich dividends can be earned not only in regard to Kashmir but in regard to other issues of interest to India. This understanding is likely to reinforce India's customary preference for avoiding overly aggressive responses to Pakistan.

If India is constrained to respond forcefully, however, the Kargil crisis suggests that covert rather than overt action might be preferable, though the fear of being embarrassed by the superior surveillance capabilities of the United States (among others) sets sharp constraints on the extent to which even covert action might be pursued as a standard course of state policy. India also understands that it won Kargil at a strategic level in part because of New Delhi's effective media management and thus can be expected to continue its pursuit of a more robust perception management capability. Finally, India has recognized the necessity of taking nuclear issues more seriously. If Kargil-like operations are expected to occur with some frequency, New Delhi may be forced to consider the need to develop some strategic rapid-response capabilities as a way to deter any Pakistani brandishing of nuclear weapons.

Chapter Four

OPTIONS FOR THE FUTURE

India and Pakistan are confronted by different futures as far as Kargil-like scenarios are concerned.

Pakistan:

- Militarily, Islamabad can only afford to attempt calibrating the heat of the insurgency. This is the best of the poor choices available to Pakistan and is likely to be emphasized in accordance with the political circumstances of the day.

- Diplomatically, the peace initiative remains with India. Pakistan can only persist in its offer to participate in peace talks at any time, place, or level and pursue the benefits to its public image that may accrue from these efforts.

- In light of its failed grand strategy and increasing political insignificance, Pakistan recognizes that it must devote resources to economic and social development. However, it will prepare to defend itself conventionally and with weapons of mass destruction (WMD) against possible Indian aggression, the trade-offs between defense and development remaining relatively unresolved.

India:

- India is unlikely to engage Pakistan "substantively" over Kashmir unless there is a larger strategic motivation to do so—even though it will eventually do so "procedurally." This means that even though New Delhi may resume "talks" with Islamabad on a variety of issues, including Kashmir, there will be no real substitute for the Indian pursuit of internal solutions to the Kashmir problem.

- India will undertake confidence-building efforts with Pakistan in order to enable Islamabad to sell domestically the concessions that New Delhi believes Pakistan will eventually have to make. India will seek to create a hospitable bilateral environment to help Pakistan achieve this aim.

- India will make a variety of military investments to improve its tactical position along the LOC. These include improvements in intelligence gathering, infrastructure, and rapid-response capabilities in Kashmir. India will also seek to develop military options that allow it to inflict costs upon the Pakistani Army at the LOC and beyond if required, but will be continually limited in the exercise of these options by both the political circumstances of the day and the necessity of preserving international support.

PAKISTAN'S PERSPECTIVE

Pakistan Will Seek to Calibrate the Heat of the Insurgency—But Risks Losing Control Over the Process at Great Cost to the Pakistani State

High-level political and military stakeholders as well as key non-state actors in Pakistan believe that Islamabad's future options are quite limited. Most interlocutors indicated that while Kargil-like situations are certainly not preferred, Pakistan's only realistic military option in the future is to continue seeking to calibrate the heat of the insurgency. Many in the Pakistani government and most in the military believe that this is a low-cost strategy by which Indian security forces in Kashmir and elsewhere can be tied up effortlessly. It imposes high costs on India in terms of the military manpower and logistics investments needed to sustain the counterinsurgency grid.

Leaders of key non-state organizations in Pakistan raised the possibility that if India continues its "intransigence," the APHC will no longer be able to influence the militants who want to attack targets outside Kashmir. (This view, while understandable, obviously exaggerates the influence that the APHC has over the more militant jihadi groups, but this fact was not addressed by any of our interlocutors.)

Well-placed Pakistani journalists indicated that the mujahideen already have an interest in pursuing targets in India's information technology (IT) centers and in other key cities that India values in terms of symbolism, tourism, and foreign direct investment. Attacking these centers of gravity is thought to impose on India significant political costs that would force New Delhi to pursue a softer strategy in resolving the Kashmir dispute.

At any rate, it is not clear how cognizant Islamabad is of "the delicate balance of instability"[1] required for the success of this strategy. It is obviously well understood that this strategy produces a de facto state of war with India. What is less well understood is that the success of this strategy requires Islamabad to inflict high enough costs on New Delhi *without* provoking it into unleashing punitive reprisals. Whether Islamabad can "calibrate" the insurgency so successfully remains an open question. In any event, this strategy continually carries within itself the possibility of conventional conflict stemming "from deliberate Indian retaliation, India's efforts to play tit-for-tat, or inadvertent action, miscalculation, or misperception on both sides."[2]

While the balance of instability is one risk posed by Pakistan's asymmetric strategy, there are other costs that appear to be discounted by Pakistan's leadership. First, the very nature of the jihadi activities besmirches Pakistan's already poor reputation and reinforces the image of India as a front-line state against Islamic terrorism. Second, Pakistan's reliance upon mujahideen and jihadi *tanzeems* to pursue its low-intensity war with India exacerbates the "principal-agent" problems inherent in this strategy in that Islamabad can never ensure that these groups will conduct themselves in a way that comports with Pakistan's larger interests both domestically and abroad. There are several dimensions to this concern.

First, these organizations have their own political agendas—which are often at variance with Pakistan's own interests or even the interests of the Kashmiris. For instance, most Pakistanis *and* Kashmiris are not receptive to the aspirations of these groups for an Islamic

---

[1]Ashley J. Tellis, *Stability in South Asia* (Santa Monica, California: RAND, 1997), p. 44.
[2]Ibid.

(Sunni) Pakistan, which would include Kashmir. Moreover, many of the jihadi groups have ambitions that go well beyond Kashmir: extremist groups like the Lashkar-e-Taiba, the Jaish-e-Mohammad, and the Harkat-ul-Ansar view themselves as being in the vanguard of a worldwide Islamist resurgence, which requires for its success the progressive destruction first of India itself, followed by Israel, and finally the United States. Given the momentum these groups have already attained in pursuit of such political objectives, it is far from obvious that Pakistan can simply shut them down even if it were to, however remotely, try.

Second, these groups are very sensitive to any developments that bear on a potential resolution of the Kashmir problem. Consequently, if they were to conclude that Pakistan has become a "Kashmir Farosh" (literally, has sold out Kashmir), they could aim their jihadi sights on Pakistan itself. Even today, these groups pose a palpable law-and-order problem, and it is not obvious that Pakistan could contend with any expanded violence with its currently constrained resources.

Third, because of the prominence these groups have attained by virtue of their importance in Pakistan's prosecution of its LIC strategy in Kashmir and because of the revisionist notions of jihad's significance to Islam proper, protests from more-moderate Muslims are effectively silenced by fear or indifference. This gives the *tanzeems* considerable leeway with respect to operations domestically.

The Peace Initiative Is Believed to Lie with India

Pakistan will pursue stratagems that give the appearance of pursuing peace for at least two reasons. First, it must cobble together some semblance of standing within the comity of nations. Second, according to several Pakistani interlocutors, some stakeholders in Pakistan believe in the necessity of a political solution—even if this political solution is thought to be hastened by continued prosecution of LIC in Kashmir. However, all of these interviewees believed that Pakistan's diplomatic options are extremely limited and that India will in effect set the terms and the pace of peace. Within these constraints, Pakistan can be expected to continue to push the envelope of peace initiated by India and will continue the present course that calls for dialog at any time, any place, and any level. However, it remains unclear whether Pakistan truly wants to pursue peace or simply wants to appear to be pursuing peace.

It must be acknowledged that the Pakistani Army has a number of incentives to prefer the status quo. First, with the current, presumedly low-cost strategy, Pakistan ties up many hundreds of thousands of troops in India's counterinsurgency grid. It is far preferable, from a Pakistani military point of view, to have these troops in Jammu and Kashmir—where they pose a minimal threat to Pakistan—than in the Punjab or Rajasthan—where they could in fact become serious objects of concern.

Second, the ongoing Kashmir problem legitimizes continued high defense expenditures in Pakistan and preserves the bureaucratic primacy of the military. Pursuing a durable peace with India brings several benefits to the country as a whole but embodies high costs for the military as an institution. Pakistan's calculus in this regard is highly complex and renders intractable an analysis of Islamabad's true interest in resolving the Kashmir problem.

Third, it is not clear that Pakistan can undertake the difficult and costly decisions that would enable it to participate meaningfully in a robust peace process. Given the problematic legitimacy of the current government, the weaknesses of Pakistan's political parties, and the continuous failures of civilian and military regimes in Pakistan, there is currently no leadership capable of making the politically difficult decision to shift Pakistan's attention, resources, and national aspirations away from Kashmir.

Fourth, Pakistan has deep suspicion and distrust of India's peace overtures. Kashmiri organizations within Pakistan, as well as the retired and uniformed military, are dubious that the various Indian cease-fire offers in Kashmir have any implications for peace. Some of their reservations are as follows:

- The cease-fire is thought to be a way to provide a much-needed breather for India's "exhausted" troops, which may afford India the opportunity to reconfigure its force structure for a limited aims war. This view derives, confusingly, from two beliefs: that India is suffering manpower problems as a result of its counterinsurgency efforts and that it is interested in fighting limited aims wars.

- Many interlocutors explained that during the cease-fire, the mujahideen become more easily identified and targeted for elimination. Thus, they fear that the Indian cease-fires in Kashmir simply provide an opportunity to hollow out the mujahideen.

- Many Pakistani interlocutors also argued that the Indian Army simply swaps uniforms with the police forces during a cease-fire, in effect allowing India to continue killing without violating the announced stand-down of forces.

- Other interviewees feared that India is using the cease-fire to split the militants and create division amongst their ranks. In particular, it is believed that India wants to create fissures between Kashmiri fighters and the "guest militants."

- Finally, some interviewees believed that the cease-fire will vitiate the momentum of the mujahideen because it is difficult to begin fighting again once the mujahideen have returned home. This concern becomes more salient the longer a cease-fire continues.

Pakistan is thus ambivalent, at best, about India's intentions and consequently can be expected to prepare for peace (or at least give the appearance of doing so) while also preparing for the possibility that India is really serving its own self-interests.

Pakistan's Weaknesses Make It Increasingly Politically Irrelevant, and Its Grand Strategy Offers No Exits

Pakistan's inability to protect its interests vis-à-vis the international community and particularly India stems from the fact that its economic and political weaknesses increasingly make it strategically irrelevant.[3] As discussed throughout this analysis, Kargil was significant because it demonstrated to Pakistan that it has virtually no cachet in the community of nations. Its weak economy is subject to the vicissitudes of multilateral funding institutions. Its government has become widely criticized for its association with odious regimes

---

[3]For example, see "Kargil: Where Do We Go from Here." See also Abbas Rashid, "Raising the Ante in Kashmir"; Imtiaz Gul, "Retreat Dictated by Economic Compulsions"; Shafqaat Mahmood, "Losing the Peace"; Mahdi Masud, "Kargil Crisis: A Balance Sheet"; Aziz Siddiqui, "In the Aftermath of 'Jihad'"; "Prime Minister Explains."

such as the Taliban and for providing training and support to militants fighting in India. It has been unable to sell the case that its interests in Kashmir are legitimate and are responsive to India's human rights violations in the region. And it has been unable to convincingly corroborate its claims about India's incursions across the LOC, including India's occupation of Siachen.[4]

Indeed, Kargil has seriously compromised the legitimacy of Pakistan's claims on Kashmir. Further, while India has been reasonably successful in casting itself as a responsible nuclear-weapons state, Pakistan remains a suspect nation as far as the diffusion of strategic technologies is concerned. Whereas India has remained connected to the West on the basis of its pluralist democracy, Pakistan has had difficulty developing robust democratic institutions. Irrespective of what level of resources and commitment Pakistan devotes to tackling this cluster of complex challenges, Pakistan faces an uphill battle in its struggle to remain strategically relevant.

In the face of these challenges—many of which are economic—Pakistan will persist in its plans for defense modernization, affording little hope that Pakistan can resolve the inherent tension between its economic condition and its military allocations. Moreover, there is little hope that Pakistan can undertake meaningful steps to change any of the aforementioned factors that contribute to Pakistan's irrelevance: so long as the Kashmiri cause remains the cause célèbre in Pakistan and Islamabad continues to preside over a garrison state, the painful political decisions necessary to steer the polity toward a more fruitful strategic trajectory cannot be made—to the detriment of both Pakistan's future and the cause of stability in South Asia.

INDIA'S PERSPECTIVE

India Will Pursue an Internal Solution to Kashmir

Of all the broad policy options that confront India with respect to Kashmir, New Delhi has always emphasized the pursuit of an inter-

---

[4]India's occupation of Siachen is legally ambiguous. However, to discuss the legal minutiae associated with this episode is to entirely overlook the degree to which Pakistan is immensely dissatisfied with the status quo.

nal solution—in part because the Indian nationalist understanding of the structure of the Kashmir dispute allows New Delhi no other alternatives. Prime Minister Vajpayee gambled considerable political capital in undertaking the initiative that resulted in the Lahore Declaration. This declaration, which could have provided some opportunity for bilateral discussions about Kashmir, quickly came to naught because of the Kargil war, which was probably initiated before the Lahore Declaration and viewed as cynical duplicity in India. Consequently, even the very modest Indian inclination to resolve the Kashmir problem with an acknowledgment of Pakistan's equity in the situation has now been vitiated. After Kargil, however, even the more dovish elements in the Indian political spectrum have become wary of pursuing discussions with Pakistan. India thus will redouble its efforts to pursue an internal solution, and while there may emerge a larger strategic purpose in engaging Pakistan bilaterally on this issue (i.e., if Pakistan is seen as willing to accept, rationalize, or legitimize the status quo with some modification), this engagement will be pursued primarily to create preconditions for the success of the internal solution.

India's internal solution centers on negotiating with the Kashmiris in order to arrive at acceptable terms for the cessation of violence and the resuscitation of a political process within the larger framework of the Indian constitution. To further this objective, New Delhi will continue its efforts to co-opt the Kashmiri moderates while marginalizing the extremists. Further, New Delhi will seek to woo the more moderate elements within the APHC, as well as other political forces in Kashmir.[5] India is also likely to let the APHC formally discuss Kashmiri issues with Pakistan (which is already occurring anyway through clandestine means) if this facilitates communicating to Islamabad the boundary of practical solutions.

While pursuing negotiations with the Kashmiris, India will continue its strategy of marginalizing Pakistan internationally. Throughout the many Indian cease-fires in Kashmir, India has done much to cast Pakistan as the laggard. For example, Indian Army Chief S. Padman-

---

[5]The public manifestation of "wooing the Kashmiris" may change frequently. However, the particular manifestation of these overtures is not relevant; rather, the point of interest is that the only palatable option to New Delhi is to negotiate a separate peace with the Kashmiris.

abhan has made numerous public assertions that Pakistan reduced infiltration across the LOC in November and December 2000, but he contested Pakistan's assertion of having pulled out troops from the LOC and from the international border in Jammu and Kashmir.[6] Consequently, India will continue to exhort Pakistan to play a positive role in resolving the Kashmir problem even as India seeks to avoid making discussions with Islamabad the centerpiece of its solution for restoring peace in the disputed state.

Even as it pursues this strategy, as will be discussed below, India will be prepared to make infiltration increasingly difficult by plugging up the border and through aggressive prosecution of LIC within Kashmir.

India Will Seek a Hospitable Bilateral Environment

Eventually India will return to its long-standing offer of engaging in "composite talks" with Pakistan. Through this process, within which the Lahore Declaration may be understood, India will pursue the normalization of bilateral relations on a wide range of key issues such as visas, cross-cultural exchanges, trade, and commerce. Kashmir would thus be discussed primarily in the context of other confidence-building measures that will have to be implemented.

The larger Indian goal in this process is to provide a positive atmosphere so that the relevant Pakistani leadership can build public support for the concessions that Islamabad will eventually have to make. From India's perspective, the only acceptable concession is the conversion of the LOC (perhaps with some modifications) into a de jure international border, a fact privately admitted in interviews at the highest levels of the Indian government. Such a concession, if offered in the context of a lasting agreement with Pakistan, would ipso facto involve India's renunciation of its present claims over "Pakistan occupied Kashmir" and the Northern Territories.

Several issues bear on the success of this approach. First, what type of regime can convince the Pakistani polity that peace dividends will accrue to Pakistan domestically and internationally if a suitably

---

[6]See "Army Chief for Extension of Truce Beyond R-Day."

modified LOC is ratified as the international border? Certainly a military leader may not be in a position to pursue this option if such a move is perceived as discrediting the institution of the Army itself. No military leader, including Musharraf, is likely to take on the onus of selling such a solution back home, even if a military leader is in fact best situated to sell such a concession. In all probability, the Pakistani military leadership would prefer a civilian leader to make this concession and take the flak that would ensue (when it reaches the conclusion that such a concession is in fact necessary). Second, it remains unclear how Pakistan could or would sell this idea given that the Pakistani public has been told for fifty years that, come hell or high water, Kashmir will be liberated from India. Third, even if a solution centering on a suitably modified LOC as the international boundary is sold to the majority, how will such a compromise be received by the jihadi and other radicalized elements in Pakistani domestic politics?

Whereas there is wide belief on both sides of the border that this will be a hard settlement for Pakistan, stakeholders in both India and Pakistan acknowledge that the Indian polity would have little problem accepting this as a solution so long as it is truly a means of buying a *permanent* peace in South Asia.

India Will Enhance Its Operational Capabilities and May Contemplate More-Aggressive Actions Along the LOC

Kargil has amply demonstrated India's military vulnerability along the porous LOC and has illuminated the need for enhanced vigilance. While it is generally agreed that more attention and resources ought to be dedicated along the LOC and within Kashmir, effectively operationalizing security solutions is a complex undertaking.

The Kargil crisis highlighted the need for new surveillance and warning systems to augment India's existing capabilities. India has "authorized a new cluster of technology initiatives focused on rapidly increasing India's imaging capabilities through the acquisition of both high-endurance unmanned aerial vehicles (UAVs) and new space-based systems together with their associated ground-based control centers and image processing facilities."[7]

The Indian Air Force (IAF) received considerable attention as it engaged in OPERATION VIJAY. The poor showing of some of the aircraft used during the operation highlighted the need for more-advanced electronic warfare, early warning equipment, modern ammunitions, and joint institutions for planning, coordination, and operations. An unidentified senior IAF official interviewed by Rediff on The NeT expressed how the Kargil operations exposed the inadequacy of Indian equipment: "But for the first time we are feeling the pinch of waging a high-altitude war in Kargil because we are faced with an acute lack of modern electronic warfare. . . .We [the IAF] have been demanding the induction of state-of-the-art fighter planes into the IAF for many years now. We hope the government will agree to our demands after the Kargil operations."[8] The IAF's poor showing in Kargil can be attributed to various factors: the IAF never seriously planned or practiced for high-altitude operations, and there are large and still unresolved systemic problems within the force, including problems associated with manning, training, and equipment.

The *Kargil Review Committee Report* highlights the key technological and structural improvements necessary for the Indian intelligence community to consider. Among the elements requiring attention are the flow of intelligence from tactical elements to strategic agencies, the analysis of the many pieces of information coming in from different sectors, the communication among the various agencies, and the necessary technological upgrades for early warning surveillance equipment. Effective strategic warning is also imperative, and it requires not only an investment in better technology, but also a com-

---

[7]Ashley J. Tellis, *India's Emerging Nuclear Posture: Between Recessed Deterrent and Ready Arsenal* (Santa Monica, California: RAND, forthcoming). Specific information regarding the approved technology as well as India's extant capabilities is also included in this forthcoming work, as well as in "Israeli UAVs: Forces of the Future," *Vayu Aerospace Review*, IV/2000, pp. 50–52; "Imaging Capability," *Aviation Week & Space Technology*, November 22, 1999, p. 17; "'Spy Satellite' Launch by Year-End," *The Hindu*, July 2, 2000.

[8]George Iype, "Kargil Exposes an Ill-Equipped IAF," Rediff on The NeT, June 15, 1999 (available at http://www.rediff.com/news/1999/jun/15iype.htm).

mitment to better intelligence assessment and disseminating procedures at the highest political and diplomatic levels.[9]

Given these assessments, the operational impact of the Kargil war has been a renewed Indian commitment to maintaining a robust forward defense. The Indian military is actively looking for technical means to secure this objective, including personnel sensors, communications interception gear, UAVs, and enhanced satellite surveillance equipment. Additionally, India will modernize its physical infrastructure in Kashmir. For example, India is likely to create a new road system to Siachen that does not come within range from the strategic heights of the Kargil-Dras sector. And finally, it will improve its rapid-response capabilities and its counterinsurgency grid system to deny the insurgents freedom of movement to the maximum extent possible.

Even as it pursues a more robust forward defense, India will also explore options that would permit it to inflict costs upon the Pakistani Army at the LOC and beyond if Kargil-like threats were seen to occur or the Pakistani Army's support for the infiltrating insurgents were to increase in intensity. Presently, Pakistan's military understands its conflict strategy to be low cost in part because it has transferred a substantial portion of these costs to the civilian population that participates in the "jihad." If the Pakistani military's support for the insurgency (or the threat of Kargil-like operations) were to increase, there would be increased incentives for India to contemplate strategies that would increase the costs borne by the Pakistani Army *directly* rather than simply by their insurgent proxies. These strategies could include a stepping up of small unit attacks on Pakistani Army positions at or along the LOC, the interdiction of rearward targets through artillery or air power, or covert attacks carried out on strategic facilities by special forces, in addition to dramatic new uses of air and naval power.

Any full-scale exercise of these options, however, would be at variance with the policy articulated in the *Kargil Review Committee Report*, which suggests that the Indian response to Pakistani incursions

---

[9]India Kargil Review Committee, *From Surprise to Reckoning: The Kargil Review Committee Report,* pp. 253–256; Ashley J. Tellis, *India's Emerging Nuclear Posture: Between Recessed Deterrent and Ready Arsenal.*

will be conservative and restrained. While this has in fact been the case historically, any upsurge in Pakistani military provocations in the aftermath of Kargil could bring a quick end to India's traditional restraint.

Within the Indian Army and in the community of retired military officers, three options for dealing with increased Pakistani provocations (including Pakistan-supported incursions along the LOC) received great attention:

- Maintaining the current, dominantly reactive approach that calls for intercepting and engaging militants after they have infiltrated.

- Hitting militants at the LOC itself while they are infiltrating (if possible) or, preferably, before they infiltrate (either at their "concentration" points in Pakistan-held Kashmir or as they are en route to the LOC).

- Interdicting Pakistani Army assets at, along, or behind the LOC at tactically shallow depths.

The first of these options calls for maintaining a more vigilant reconnaissance and surveillance presence along the LOC while plugging the holes along the boundary. This is the strategy most clearly articulated within the *Kargil Review Committee Report.* From the perspective of the Indian military, however, this option is necessary but may not be sufficient if it is read as prohibiting the targeting of militants before they have infiltrated (as is usually the case). This approach exposes Indian troops to increased threat while restricting the Indian Army from inflicting costs on the Pakistanis. The second option would be optimal from an operational, and perhaps even a political, perspective: it would permit the Indian Army to inflict significant damage on Pakistani-supported infiltrating groups through aggressive policing of the LOC while still limiting India's political exposure. The disadvantage of this option, however, is that its success requires highly effective intelligence, often sheer luck, and constant and successful small-unit patrolling along the LOC. The third option is the most aggressive of the three and thus far has been operationalized only sporadically and during periods of increased tension. The advantage of this strategy is that it imposes nontrivial costs on the Pakistani Army directly, as opposed to merely on its proxies, and it helps to render the Pakistanis psychologically vulnerable. However, it increases India's political exposure—if operationalized as the dominant strategy—and could lead to the loss of the international support that currently is available because India is viewed as a responsible state.

On balance, therefore, the first and second strategies are likely to remain the dominant authorized responses in the future. The third strategy is likely to be authorized only under conditions of great provocation: the Kargil war has demonstrated to India the value of being seen as moderate and responsible, and Indian policymakers, wishing to maintain this perception of India as a state, are likely to be extremely reluctant to authorize any strategy that would subvert this key grand strategic interest. The Indian Army, for its part, is a highly disciplined institution and thus unlikely to ever pursue such a strategy independently—that is, without explicit authorization from the national leadership. And the political costs attending such a course of action almost certainly preclude it from being adopted as an Indian response to Pakistan except under grave circumstances and then only covertly.

CONCLUSIONS

The Kargil war has conditioned Pakistani and Indian conceptions of their future choices, albeit for very different reasons. Pakistan has slowly come to appreciate the costs that it has had to endure as a result of Kargil. Pakistan is economically vulnerable, politically unstable, and internationally isolated, and has acquired the opprobrium of being viewed as a precarious, decaying, and increasingly Islamist state. The Pakistani elite finds this last perception particularly galling because most consider themselves to be *Muslim,* not Islamist. Pakistani moderates believe, however, that their political leadership and/or the military are more or less impotent against the jihadi elements, in part because of their need for them in the context of Pakistan's larger grand strategy. One interlocutor, a moderate retired general, articulated the confusion over Pakistan's destiny and the types of strategic calculus required to support this vision of Pakistan's future: "Pakistan needs to figure out whether it wants to be Jinnah's Pakistan, the Jamaat-e-Islami's Pakistan, or the Lashkar-e-Taiba's Pakistan. When it figures this out, the rest will follow."

India is not likely to give Pakistan a chance to flirt with Kargil-like scenarios in the future. New Delhi will watch the border in Kashmir and elsewhere carefully and will redouble its efforts to prevent infiltration. India understands that the most probable response from Pakistan will be efforts to calibrate the heat of the insurgency. This may entail a continuation of terrorist attacks throughout India. However, New Delhi also appreciates that this strategy redounds to Pakistan's own disadvantage—though it fears that Islamabad may in fact lose control over its proxies—and further confirms Pakistan as a sponsor of Islamist terrorism. In this struggle, India will not take international support for granted. As during Kargil, India appreciates the value of international, including U.S., support and understands that such support is highly contingent on circumstances. In this context, India realizes that military heavy-handedness in dealing with Pakistan will corrode its international reputation. Regardless of the psychological gratification that might accrue to a strategy of "giving Pakistan a bloody nose," New Delhi will continue to exhibit substantial restraint—despite an occasional lapse—precisely because it seeks to secure geopolitical goals much larger than simply humiliating Islamabad.

Chapter Five

CONCLUSION: KARGIL AND SOUTH ASIAN STABILITY

What impact has Kargil had on South Asian stability? This chapter seeks to answer this question briefly by revisiting earlier RAND work on deterrence breakdown in South Asia that was undertaken in 1994.[1] That work argued that in the foreseeable future, South Asia would experience a condition of "ugly stability"—that is, the persistence of unconventional conflicts—because conventional wars of either unlimited or limited aims had become either prohibitively costly or beyond the easy reach of both India and Pakistan for purposes of national policy. Further, owing to the presence of nuclear weapons, India and especially Pakistan would be particularly enticed to engage in various types of subconventional conflicts at the lower end of the conflict spectrum. Previous research thus adjudged war to be unlikely except under certain dramatic changes in the overall power-political balance between India and Pakistan, so the question of whether deterrence could break down merits revisitation in the aftermath of Kargil.

This chapter first summarizes some of the key arguments in support of the claim that "ugly stability" will obtain in the foreseeable future. Second, it explores whether these conclusions still hold in the post-Kargil South Asian environment. It then concludes by identifying several key issues that merit further investigation and research.

---

[1] Ashley J. Tellis, *Stability in South Asia.*

PROSPECTS FOR PEACE AND POSSIBILITIES OF WAR

Earlier RAND research on stability in South Asia argued that pre-meditated *unlimited aims* wars were not likely for at least another decade. Other things being equal, this conclusion was based mainly on the inability of both countries to achieve rapid and decisive victory within a two-to-three-week period, which is the duration of war most relevant to the subcontinent. If a war expanded beyond this time frame, it would become a painful and costly matter of attrition that would eventually redound to India's natural advantages. This is Pakistan's principal military disincentive with respect to initiating an unlimited aims conflict. Although India is not hampered by similar limitations, New Delhi is not favorably inclined to endure the varied costs of a war of attrition today. In any event, political objectives ultimately determine the improbability of unlimited aims wars in South Asia. India currently betrays little interest in subjugating or fractionating Pakistan despite the exasperation often expressed at Pakistani behavior. While some extremists in Pakistan may desire to dismember India, Pakistan simply lacks the capability to pursue this type of goal, at least through the pursuit of wars of unlimited aims.[2]

In this context, wars of *limited aims* are certainly possible in principle, because each country does have the capability to pursue this type of war. However, these conflicts too were judged to be generally unlikely in practice, in this case because fear of operational failure would interact with the concern that neither side could assure itself (a) that the war would be terminated on demand after the initial success was achieved and (b) that once initiated, the war could in fact be kept limited in aims, means, and consequences throughout the course of the campaign. This is the principal deterrent to limited aims wars, and this conclusion is likely to hold as long as both India and Pakistan have a relative military balance similar to that existing at present and so long as there is no dramatic shift in the regional balance of power.[3]

The role of nuclear capabilities in maintaining deterrence stability is analytically—though perhaps not "empirically"—unclear, because in

---

[2]Ibid., pp. 13–31.

[3]Ibid., pp. 30–31.

some sense deterrence stability is *overdetermined* by the weak conventional force capabilities of both states, the lack of political incentives to dramatically change the status quo, and the prohibitive costs of conventional warfare when viewed against both countries' economic weaknesses *as well as* their now overt nuclear capabilities. In any event, the destabilizing effects of nuclear capabilities are clearly more apparent and observable in that nuclear weapons have permitted India and particularly Pakistan to prosecute a range of unconventional conflicts at the lower end of the spectrum of violence.[4]

The incentives to prosecute unconventional conflicts in the form of state-supported terrorism or state-supported insurgency will continue to persist, in large part because conventional conflicts remain risky. As a result, South Asia will continue to experience conventional deterrence stability even though this stability will be "ugly" and will entail a high degree of subconventional and unconventional violence.[5]

IMPLICATIONS OF KARGIL FOR "UGLY STABILITY"

Since unlimited aims wars are unlikely for the various political and military reasons summarized above, and since subconventional wars are certain to persist indefinitely (again, for the reasons explored above), the critical question that merits revisitation is whether limited aims wars between India and Pakistan—the prospects of which were generally minimized in previous research except under changes in certain specific boundary conditions[6]—are likely to materialize in the future. If they are, the challenges for stability in South Asia could become quite acute, at least episodically. While subconventional and unconventional wars can entail high levels of violence and are consequently quite problematic, they do not involve an organized application of military force in the way that limited wars invariably do. Organized applications of force bring in their wake the potential for escalation both horizontally and vertically and, as a result, chal-

---

[4]Ibid., pp. 30–33.

[5]Ibid.

[6]For the circumstances under which limited wars could break out in South Asia, see Ashley J. Tellis, *Stability in South Asia*, pp. 55–59.

lenge stability in a way that subconventional violence and unconventional violence often do not.

The prospect for the outbreak of limited wars in South Asia therefore merits brief examination. How likely is limited aims war in the future? To begin with, it must be recognized that Kargil *was*, in some sense, a limited aims war in that at least one of Pakistan's objectives was to secure territory, however marginal. Of course, its other objective, to internationalize the conflict, was just as salient—if not more so—than these meager territorial ambitions. One of the principal deterrents to initiating limited aims war in South Asia is the inability to assure international intervention and the cessation of hostilities after the achievement of a state's immediate operational aims. As described in earlier chapters, Pakistan did seem to believe that the international community would intervene in a fashion both timely and consonant with Pakistan's strategic interest once it had secured its operational aims early in the conflict. Given this assumption—however flawed it was to begin with—it is no surprise that Pakistan initiated the Kargil war, because the expectation of international intervention leading to a quick termination of hostilities served in effect to remove one of the principal deterrents to the initiation of limited aims wars: the fear that, absent quick, on-demand termination of conflict, the war could spin out of control and degenerate into a major, open-ended campaign that would redound to Islamabad's disadvantage. However, one of the lessons that Pakistan *has* learned from Kargil is that such optimistic expectations of the international community's role in South Asian rivalries are unwarranted. Such a conclusion could deter Kargil-like limited aims wars in the future.

In another sense, however, Kargil can be seen as an example not of a limited aims war (in the conventional sense described in the literature) but, rather, of Pakistan pushing the envelope with respect to LIC. This reading is reinforced by the fact that Islamabad went to great lengths to disguise its participation in the war and to this day has not officially admitted its role in the initiation of the Kargil conflict.[7] To the degree that Kargil turns out to be an example of a detour in what is otherwise LIC, the explanation for deterrence failure

---

[7]See Pakistan, Ministry of Foreign Affairs, "Jammu Kashmir Dispute," at www.forisb.org/Kashmir.html.

in this event is less complicated, though it does ride on a bewildering number of peculiar assumptions that informed Pakistani decision-making with respect to this event—for example, that the presence of Pakistani forces would not be detected, and that if detected, would have no political consequences; that the Indian response to the Pakistani fait accompli would be passive and quiescent; and that the Kargil war would have little real effect on India-Pakistan relations. The cumulative effect of such peculiar assumptions renews the concerns many observers have traditionally had about the character of Pakistani decisionmaking with respect to grand strategy and about the effects of that strategy on strategic stability in South Asia.[8] Thus, while it is possible to conclude that Pakistan, having learned once again that favorable international intervention and on-demand war termination cannot be assured, is unlikely to initiate a future Kargil-like operation, the uncertainty about whether Pakistan's higher decisionmaking institutions—which, all admit, are relatively weak—can in fact internalize these lessons permanently and institutionally gives rise to legitimate fears that Islamabad (if it chooses to behave like the Bourbon monarchy that reputedly learned nothing and forgot nothing) might be tempted to replicate some facsimile of the Kargil operation in the future.

These fears are only exacerbated by the fact—underscored in this report—that Pakistan's evaluation of the consequences of Kargil is still ambiguous. Had Pakistan concluded that the Kargil operation was an outright failure, the prospects of recurrence would have been minimal. However, Pakistan's lessons learned are more complex. Even as the overall failure of the Kargil operation dominates the consciousness of many Pakistani stakeholders, several important constituencies still tend to rationalize Kargil, even if only as an afterthought, as some sort of a victory. These conceptions of victory—the brilliance of the tactical planning, the effectiveness of Pakistan's operational performance, the conflict as progenitor of India's political dialog with the Kashmiris—differ often as a result of where the constituency is located in Pakistan's state-society structure, but the "residue" of such beliefs implies the possibility that Pakistan might be tempted to carry out Kargil-like operations in the future.

---

[8]See Ahmad Faruqui, "Failure in Command: Lessons from Pakistan's India Wars," *Defense Analysis* (forthcoming).

The lingering possibility that future Kargils might arise—however remote that seems at present—is rooted ultimately in the particular dynamics of the current India-Pakistan rivalry in South Asia.

On the Pakistani side of the rivalry, the current regime is impassionedly focused on "resolving" Kashmir, and its support for the insurgency is unlikely to dissipate any time soon—*even though this policy is orthogonal to Pakistan's current endeavors to address its serious economic problems*. This support serves various purposes:

- Distracting India through the medium of subconventional and unconventional war is seen as bequeathing strategic benefits for Pakistani security.

- Supporting the insurgency has turned out to be a productive strategy for employing local and Afghan Islamists who might otherwise be tempted to turn their revolutionary zeal inward, toward Pakistan.

- The Kashmir insurgency is one of two major issues (the nuclear program being the other) that cement national solidarity and may help to legitimize military rule in the face of continuing weaknesses in the development of Pakistan's identity.

- A future "diversionary war" could be precipitated by Pakistan's domestic disarray, which is caused in part by weak institutions, civil-military discord, poor economic performance, and an infirm civil society.

Finally, Pakistan's evolving nuclear capabilities might be judged to provide effective strategic cover for an activist Kashmir policy that sanctions episodic limited aims operations if the strategic environment is in fact believed to be conducive to the initiation of such operations.

On the Indian side, New Delhi's commitment to an internal solution to the Kashmir problem creates greater incentives for Pakistan to assert its equities in the ongoing dispute through means of overt force if necessary. While the Indian conviction about the desirability of an internal solution is rooted in larger beliefs about the liberal, secular, and multiethnic nature of the Indian Union, the unwitting byproduct of pursuing such a solution will be an increased resistance on the part of Pakistan. Precisely because the positions of the two antagonists are in *absolute* conflict—because neither can sacrifice its cherished approach to the problem without subverting other equally critical political goals—the currently reigning condition of "ugly stability" in South Asia may be occasionally punctuated by episodes of "uglier stability" from time to time. In such an environment, a wide variety of Kargil-like operations could occur, each differing in scale, intensity, and consequences. But if all goes well, any such intense and episodic "crisis slide" will gradually recede to the pre-existing condition of ugly stability.[9]

The interplay of these Indian and Pakistani dynamics and the diverging trend lines in the political futures of both countries—a dissatisfied and deteriorating Pakistan vs. a confident and growing India— almost ensures that the India-Pakistan rivalry will persist, and that rivalry alone permits the possibility—however remote—that Pakistan could pursue Kargil-like operations in the future. In fact, a good argument could be made that the Kargil war itself was conditioned at least in part by the growing Pakistani recognition that India is on the verge of becoming the hegemonic state in South Asia: the closing window of opportunity represented by this fact implied the need for dramatic action at a time when the international community still shared a certain sympathy for Pakistan in the aftermath of India's May 1998 nuclear tests. In any event, even if operations on the scale and intensity of Kargil do not occur in the future, political-military crises in South Asia are likely to surface over the course of the next decade. Until Pakistan pulls out of its current economic morass, institutionalizes a stable set of responsive governing institutions, inculcates a democratic temper, cements a political identity outside of opposition to India, and acts upon the realization that Kashmir, no matter how valuable, is still not as valuable as Pakistan, the resentment, grievances, and dissatisfaction that currently drive Islamabad's Kashmir and India policies will only compel Pakistan to contemplate future Kargil-like operations, despite the fact that the full range of costs of such operations may grossly outweigh any putative benefits.

---

[9]Ashley J. Tellis, *India's Emerging Nuclear Posture: Between Recessed Deterrent and Ready Arsenal*, pp. 131–132.

AREAS REQUIRING FURTHER INVESTIGATION

Three topics requiring further investigation came to the fore in thinking through the possibilities for deterrence breakdown in the long term. The first is Pakistan's inability or unwillingness to control the jihadi elements existing within and immediately outside its territory, and the impact of these groups on Pakistan's civil society and internal security.

The second issue that emerged is the possibilities arising from India's contemplation of "limited war."[10] As thinking about limited war evolves in India, this issue merits further scrutiny. Analysts need to assess and understand the meaning of the concept and its implications for deterrence breakdown, the current state of Indian planning for limited operations, and the doctrinal changes that would be necessitated by the formal adoption of this concept, if this in fact occurs.

The third area is the likelihood that China and the United States will seek to reconfigure their bilateral relations with India. This issue has most import for the longer-term prospects of conventional deterrence breakdown insofar as it affects the incentives for India, Pakistan, and China to contemplate various kinds of dyadic wars.

---

[10]See C. Raja Mohan, "Fernandes Unveils 'Limited War' Doctrine," *The Hindu*, online edition, January 25, 2000; Anthony Davis, "When Words Hurt: No Limits on a 'Limited War'," *Asia Week*, Vol. 26, No. 12, March 31, 2000; George Fernandes, "Dynamics of Limited War," *Strategic Affairs*, online edition, October 15, 2000, available at http://www.stratmag.com/issueOct-15/page07.htm. See also V.R. Raghavan, "Limited War and Strategic Liability," *The Hindu*, February 2, 2000.

REFERENCES

Akbar, M., "Time for Sober Reflection," *The Dawn*, July 22, 1999.

Ali, Mayed, "China Pledges to Stand by Pakistan in All Circumstances," *The News*, June 30, 1999.

Amin, Shahid M., "Kargil: The Unanswered Questions II—Time to Shed Illusions," *The Dawn*, July 26, 1999.

"Army Chief for Extension of Truce Beyond R-Day," *The Hindustan Times*, January 12, 2001.

"Assurance from Russia" [editorial], *The Hindustan Times*, May 30, 1999.

Baruah, Amit, "Pakistan Wants International Attention," *The Hindu*, May 28, 1999.

Baruah, Amit, "U.S. Asks Pak to Pull Out Intruders," *The Hindu*, June 25, 1999.

Bearak, Barry, "Pakistani Journalists May Face Death for Publishing Letter," *New York Times*, February 19, 2001.

"Before It Gets Any Worse" [editorial], *The Dawn*, May 27, 1999.

Bhandara, M.P., "On the Edge of the Precipice," *The Dawn*, July 21, 1999.

Bose, Sumantra, "Kashmir: Sources of Conflict, Dimensions of Peace," *Survival*, Vol. 41, No. 3, Autumn 1999, pp. 149–171.

Chengappa, Raj, "Pakistan Threatened India with Nuclear Attack: Army Chief," *The Newspaper Today,* January 12, 2001.

Chengappa, Raj, *Weapons of Peace: The Secret Story of India's Quest to Be a Nuclear Power* (New Delhi, India: Harper Collins, 2000).

Chibber, M.L., "Siachen—The Untold Story," *Indian Defence Review,* January 1990

"Clinton Appreciates India's Restraint," *The Hindu,* June 15, 1999.

Davis, Anthony, "When Words Hurt: No Limits on a 'Limited War'," *Asia Week,* Vol. 26, No. 12, March 31, 2000.

"Defusing the Crisis" [editorial], *The Dawn,* June 5, 1999.

"Delhi Plans Publicity Blitz to Expose Direct Role of Pakistan," *The Hindustan Times,* May 30, 1999.

Durrani, Asad, "Beyond Kargil," *The News International Pakistan,* July 9, 1999.

Ejaz, Manzur, "An Unlikely Beneficiary of the Kargil Crisis," *The News International Pakistan,* July 11, 1999.

Evans, Alexander, "Reducing Tension Is Not Enough," *The Washington Quarterly,* Vol. 24, No. 2, 2001, pp. 181–193.

Fernandes, George, "Dynamics of Limited War," *Strategic Affairs* (online edition), October 15, 2000 (available at http://www.stratmag.com/issueOct-15/page07.htm).

"G-8 Can Now Play Proactive Role in Indo-Pak Conflict," *The Hindustan Times Online Edition,* June 22, 1999.

"G-8 Communiqué," June 1999.

Gauhar, Altaf, "Four Wars, One Assumption," *The Nation,* September 5, 1999.

"German Intelligence Says Osama Is Involved in the Kashmir Crisis," *The Asian Age,* June 16, 1999.

Gul, Imtiaz, "Retreat Dictated by Economic Compulsions," *The News International Pakistan,* July 10, 1999.

"Hope in China" [editorial], *The News*, June 30, 1999.

"Imaging Capability," *Aviation Week & Space Technology*, November 22, 1999, p. 17.

"India and the U.S. After Kargil," *The Hindu*, June 24, 1999.

"India Determined Not to Lose More Territory: PM," *The Times of India*, March 1, 1999.

India Kargil Review Committee, *From Surprise to Reckoning: The Kargil Review Committee Report* (New Delhi: Sage Publications, 2000).

"Israeli UAVs: Forces of the Future," *Vayu Aerospace Review*, IV/2000, pp. 50–52.

"It's My Dream to Resolve Kashmir Issue: Musharraf," *The Times of India Online*, February 10, 2001.

Iype, George, "Kargil Exposes an Ill-Equipped IAF," Rediff on The NeT, June 15, 1999 (available at http://www.rediff.com/news/1999/jun/15iype.htm).

"J&K's Return to Home Signals Change in Policy," *The Hindustan Times Online Edition*, May 26, 1998.

"Jihadis Cannot Be Stopped from Collecting Fund [sic]: Court," *The Times of India Online*, February 22, 2001.

Kanwal, Gurmeet, "Nawaz Sharif's Damning Disclosures," *The Pioneer*, August 16, 2000.

"Kargil Infiltrators Are Fundamentalists: Russia," *The Hindustan Times*, May 29, 1999.

"Kargil: Where Do We Go From Here" [letter to the editor], *The Dawn*, July 10, 1999.

"Kashmir Is Not Kosovo," *The Pioneer*, May 30, 1999.

Katyal, K.K., "Pak Wooing China," *The Hindu*, June 10, 1999.

Khajuria, K.S., "Kargil Task Not an Easy One," *The Times of India*, May 29, 1999.

Khan, M. Ilyas, "Life After Kargil," *The Herald,* July 2000, pp. 24–30.

Khan, Tanyir Ahmed, "Understanding China Is Vital," *The Dawn,* July 6, 1999.

Krishnaswami, Sridhar, "Pull Back Forces, Clinton Tells Sharif," *The Hindu,* June 16, 1999.

Krishnaswami, Sridhar, "Zinni Mission to Pak, Very Productive," *The Hindu,* June 29, 1999.

Lahore Declaration. Available at U.S. Institute of Peace Web site: http://www.usip.org/library/pa/ip/ip_lahore19990221.html.

"The Line of Crisis," *The Indian Express,* June 29, 1999.

Madan, Vijay, "Population Terrain—The Neglected Factor of Counter-Insurgency Operations," *Indian Defence Review,* Vol. 12, No. 2, April–June, 1997.

Mahmood, Afzal, "China's Cautious Approach," *The Dawn,* July 4, 1999.

Mahmood, Afzal, "Defusing the Tension," *The Dawn,* June 5, 1999.

Mahmood, Afzal, "Seeing Kargil in Perspective," *The Dawn,* July 18, 1999.

Mahmood, Afzal, "Ties with China in Perspective," *The Dawn,* June 29, 1999.

Mahmood, Shafqaat, "Losing the Peace," *The News International Pakistan,* July 10, 1999.

Masud, Mahdi, "Kargil Crisis: A Balance Sheet," *The Dawn,* July 16, 1999.

Mazari, Shireen M., "Kargil: Misguided Perceptions," Pakistan Institute for Air Defence Studies, n.d. (available at www.piads.com.pk/users/piads/mazari1.html).

Mazari, Shireen M., "Re-Examining Kargil," *Defence Journal* (online version), June 2000.

Merchant, D.P., "Peacekeeping in Somalia: An Indian Experience," *Army & Defence Quarterly Journal*, Vol. 126, April 1996, pp. 134–141.

Mohan, C. Raja, "China Unlikely to Adopt Anti-India Posture," *The Hindu*, June 11, 1999.

Mohan, C. Raja, "Fernandes Unveils 'Limited War' Doctrine," *The Hindu* (online edition), January 25, 2000.

Mohan, C. Raja, "Will U.S. Match Words with Deeds?" *The Hindu*, June 26, 1999.

Nanda, Ravi, *Kargil: A Wakeup Call* (New Delhi: Lancer Books, 1999).

Naqvi, M.B., "Looking Beyond Kargil," *The Dawn*, July 19, 1999.

"Nawas Was Bypassed, Feel Western Experts," *The Pioneer,* May 29, 1999.

"A One Side Approach Will Not Work," *The Dawn*, June 26, 1999.

"Pak Ploy to Escalate War, Draw Global Attention," *The Pioneer*, June 11, 1999.

"Pak Sends Mutilated Bodies Ahead of Aziz," *Indian Express*, June 11, 1999.

"Pakistan Crossed the LOC Says UN Chief," *The Hindu*, May 31, 1999.

"Pakistan's Dilemma," *The Hindustan Times*, June 30, 1999.

"Pakistan's Plan Backfires," *The Pioneer*, June 25, 1999.

"Pakistan Vows Tough Action Against Extremists," *The Times of India Online*, February 13, 2001.

Pegasus, "Insurgency and Counter-Insurgency: The Anatomy of an Insurgent Movement and Counter Measures," *Indian Defence Review*, Vol. 1, No. 1, January 1996.

"Playing with Fire" [editorial], *The Dawn*, May 30, 1999.

"PM's China Visit" [editorial], *The Dawn*, June 29, 1999.

"Prime Minister Explains" [editorial], *The Dawn*, July 14, 1999.

Radyuhin, Vladimir, "Moscow Backs Operation Against Intruders," *The Hindu*, May 28, 1999.

Raghavan, V.R., "Limited War and Strategic Liability," *The Hindu*, February 2, 2000.

Rajain, Arpit, "India's Political and Diplomatic Response to the Kargil Crisis," unpublished working paper planned for publication in P.R. Chari and Maj. Gen. Ashok Krishna (eds.), *Kargil: The Tables Turned* (New Delhi: Manohar, 2001), pp. 181–203.

Raman, B., "Is Osama bin Laden in Kargil?" *The Indian Express*, May 26, 1999.

Rashid, Abbas, "Raising the Ante in Kashmir," *The News International Pakistan*, July 2, 1999.

Ray, Arjun, *Kashmir Diary: Psychology of Militancy* (New Delhi: Manas Publications, 1997).

Reddy, B. Muralidhar, "Pak Vows Tough Measures Against 'Jihadi' Outfits," *The Hindu*, February 13, 2001.

Reddy, B. Muralidhar, "Sattar Wants Tripartite Talks Before Ramzan," *The Hindu*, December 5, 2000.

"Resume Talks, China Tells Sharif," *The Hindu*, June 29, 1999.

Sarkar, Bhaskar, *Kargil War: Past, Present, and Future* (New Delhi: Lancer Publishers, 1999).

Sattar, Abdul, "Crisis with Deep Roots," *The News International Pakistan*, June 13, 1999.

"Security Council Hands Off Kargil," *The Statesman*, May 30, 1999.

Shafi, Kamram, "Friendless in Kashmir," *The News International Pakistan*, June 21, 1999.

Shamin, Arif, "War on the Net," *The News,* July 11, 1999.

"Sharif, ISI Uninvolved, by George!" *The Hindustan Times*, May 29, 1999.

"Show Restraint: China," *The Pioneer,* May 28, 1999.

Siddiqui, Aziz, "Downhill from Kargil," *The Dawn,* June 29, 1999.

Siddiqui, Aziz, "In the Aftermath of 'Jihad'," *The Dawn,* July 11, 1999.

Singh, Jasjit, *Kargil 1999: Pakistan's Fourth War for Kashmir* (New Delhi: Knowledge World, 1999).

"'Spy Satellite' Launch by Year-End," *The Hindu,* July 2, 2000.

Swami, Parveen, *The Kargil War* (New Delhi: LeftWord Books, 1999), p. 19.

"Taliban Are Waiting to Launch Jehad in Kashmir," *The Asian Age,* June 16, 1999.

"Talks at Last" [editorial], *The Dawn,* June 10, 1999.

"Taming Pakistan," *The Times of India,* June 26, 1999.

Tellis, Ashley J., "The Changing Political-Military Environment: South Asia," in Zalmay Khalilzad et al., *The United States and Asia: Toward a New U.S. Strategy and Force Posture* (Santa Monica, California: RAND, 2001), pp. 218–224.

Tellis, Ashley J., *India's Emerging Nuclear Posture: Between Recessed Deterrent and Ready Arsenal* (Santa Monica, Calif.: RAND, forthcoming).

Tellis, Ashley J., *Stability in South Asia* (Santa Monica, California: RAND, 1997).

"U.S. Rejects Pak Claims on LOC Violations," *The Times of India,* May 28, 1999.

Varma, K.J.M., "Pakistan to Airlift Tents, Blankets for Gujarat Quake Victims," rediff.com, January 29, 2001.

Wilson, John, "Enough. Now Teach Them a Lesson," *The Pioneer,* June 11, 1999.

Wirsing, Robert G., "The Siachen Dispute: Can Diplomacy Untangle It?" *Indian Defence Review,* July 1991.